St. Francis
and the
Foolishness of God

St. Francis
and the
Foolishness of God

Revised Edition

Marie Dennis
Cynthia Moe-Lobeda
Joseph Nangle, OFM
Stuart Taylor

ORBIS BOOKS
Maryknoll, New York 10545

The publishing arm of the Maryknoll Fathers and Brothers, Orbis seeks to explore the global dimensions of the Christian faith and mission, to invite dialogue with diverse cultures and religious traditions, and to serve the cause of reconciliation and peace. The books published reflect the views of their authors and do not represent the official position of the Maryknoll Society. To learn more about Maryknoll and Orbis Books, please visit our website at www.maryknollsociety.org.

Revised edition published by Orbis Books, Box 302, Maryknoll, NY 10545-0302.

Manufactured in the United States of America.
Manuscript editing and typesetting by Joan Weber Laflamme.

Library of Congress Cataloging-in-Publication Data

St. Francis and the foolishness of God / Marie Dennis, Cynthia Moe-Lobeda, Joseph Nangle, O.F.M., Stuart Taylor. — REVISED EDITION.
    pages cm
    Includes bibliographical references.
    ISBN 978-1-62698-108-9 (pbk.)
    1. Francis, of Assisi, Saint, 1182–1226—Meditations. 2. Church and social problems—Catholic Church—Meditations. 3. Social justice. I. Dennis, Marie, joint author.
BX4700.F6S6563 2015
271'.302—dc23

2014039217

Contents

Preface to the Revised Edition

Twenty-plus years ago the witness of St. Francis of Assisi brought us together to tell again his story for our time and place. The profound appreciation for St. Francis that we shared and our commitment to the faith-based peace and justice movement in the United States prompted us to bring the life and witness of St. Francis into conversation with the challenges of faithful discipleship in the contemporary world.

Francis can teach us what it means now to follow Christ in radical discipleship. He has amazing relevance to the complex dimensions of our current global reality. The great themes of his life speak volumes to us now: his encounter with people on the margins of society and his rejection of war; the commitment of early Franciscan communities to nonviolent solidarity; his intimate friendship with Clare and respect for her own calling; his crossing over the great divide between the Christian and Muslim worlds; his contemplative practice; and above all, his ecological vision so beautifully expressed in the Canticle of Creation. All of these themes make Francis an exemplary follower of Jesus. In his life we catch sight of the new human being formed by the Spirit of God to face and address the challenges of the twenty-first and future centuries.

St. Francis continues to be a transforming spiritual presence for us and, we are sure, for countless "Franciscans" around the world—men and women of every ethnicity, culture, and faith tradition who find inspiration in Francis. It is to them that we offer this new version of the story.

Since *St. Francis and the Foolishness of God* was first published, the reality of the world in which we live has changed in significant ways, both positive and negative, and Francis's message seems even more relevant and prophetic.

In many ways the situation of the world is more perilous than before. The end of the Cold War failed to produce the hoped-for peace dividend. Terrorist attacks in the United States on September 11, 2001, provoked a seemingly endless "war on terrorism" and, with it, the polarized encounter between Christianity and Islam. Francis's relationship with the Sultan points in a very different direction.

At the same time, an increasingly globalized economy, a rise in inequality, and a proliferation of small arms bred increased violence, even as a new generation of faith-based communities deepened their analysis of the complexities of the global economy and began to discover linkages with communities in very different contexts around the globe. A yearning for peace and nonviolence, which is reinforced by the story of Francis, began to grow.

Particularly deadly for people already marginalized by poverty, the reality of climate change threatening the future of life on earth crashed through to the global consciousness. Across this planet there appears to be a cosmological awakening that has engendered increased awareness of the universe story and a deep reflection on the place of the human as part of earth community. In many ways this growing awareness echoes the insights of Francis about our relationship with the rest of creation.

All this, positive and negative alike, underlines the relevance of the original impulse—to look at St. Francis as a figure who challenges us and speaks to our condition in so many ways.

We, the authors, also have changed in these twenty years. Our horizons have expanded beyond the Latin American countries that first touched our hearts, and we have been challenged by the growing complexity of many situations and issues as we have continued on the discipleship journey. As the wars came to an end and overt repression in Latin America began to diminish, we were called to probe deeply the roots of economic injustice, to witness vastly different cultural contexts, and to embrace the African continent and the Middle East. We were witnesses to different manifestations of violence and war, explored more seriously the intersection of peace and justice, recognized the ongoing reality of white racism in our society and our world, and began to understand the nuances of nonviolence. We began to see with increasing clarity the deep relationality of everything in the universe and to understand better the amazing depth of Francis's spirituality.

Then Jorge Mario Bergoglio, a Jesuit from Argentina, was elected pope and chose the name Francis. By his integrity, simple lifestyle, and commitment to poor and marginalized people, Pope Francis immediately caught the attention of a frequently cynical world and gave powerful witness to the compelling vision of the saint whose name he assumed. Elected in the Catholic tradition, Francis's witness was embraced by people of many different faith traditions who were weary of scandal and hungry for authentic religious expression.

Inspired by the renewed hope that Pope Francis's words and witness have brought to a tired world, and believing that his message mirrors the message of St. Francis, we have updated a bit our little book, *St. Francis and the Foolishness of God*. Some of the changes we have introduced respond to the new signs of the times in which we now live, a few of which are described above. Others reflect new scholarship on the life of St. Francis and the influences on his early biographers. Robert Moses's book, *The Saint and the Sultan*, is one example. Yet other changes suggest a more critical reading of the Poverello—discerning, for example, in the Canticle of Creation a gender bias that was assumed in fourteenth-century Italy but is not acceptable in our times.

We hope this new version of our book will help the reader follow the lead of two good men named Francis—one from eight hundred years ago and the other from our own times—on the discipleship journey.

Introduction

Narrative Theology

Throughout the history of the Franciscan family, whenever there has been a crisis, a shaking of the foundations in church and society, a new story of Francis has emerged. As each historical crisis challenged Franciscans to reclaim their identity and mission, the story of Francis was retold in the community in order to understand how the charism of Francis could be applied and appropriated in the new, contemporary context. In our own times the whole church again faces a major crisis: Christians of all denominations are returning to our traditions to claim resources that can help us redefine our identity as people of faith and our mission in the world. It is time once again to tell the story of Francis.

In every generation the stories of Francis have been used as formation documents to instruct and prepare new members of the order. These stories helped form new generations of Franciscans seeking to be faithful to their vocation in situations that were very different from those faced by Francis or the first friars. These narratives formed the cohesive center of the communities in which they were told. We believe that God is calling a new generation of Franciscans, one that transcends denominational lines in the church.

We chose to tell stories of Francis in the format of this book because we are convinced that stories can be more effective than doctrinal statements in communicating the truth. Stories and the images they evoke engage the life of a reader. As we read, we imaginatively enter into the landscape of a story. The meaning of the story is found not in doctrine to be understood by the head, but in images to be embraced by the heart.

A story is a powerful medium because it resembles the very nature of human experience. Our lives are meaningful to the degree to which we are able to weave all of our life experience into a story of some kind. A story with plot, characters, action, discourse, and location is the structure of human experience. Because of this, a story has the power to interpret human reality in profound ways. We tell the stories of Francis to initiate a conversation between each text and our own context, a dialogue between our story and the story of Francis. Thus in every chapter we provide what we call a personal cultural history exercise: a series of questions that can be used for journaling, reflection, and discussion that we hope will enable the reader to dig more fruitfully into the rich soil of his or her own culture. Similarly, we provide social analysis reflections and exercises to deepen our understanding of how the Franciscan story can be creatively appropriated in our own socioeconomic context.

What can be said about the stories of Francis can also be said about the scriptures included in each chapter: these too are stories that challenge us with images of a radical alternative. These stories have the ability to disturb as well as to animate and energize the reader. When a story is read, in a very real sense it is not the reader who interprets the story, but the story that interprets the reader. We may read a story from the world of Francis (or from a Gospel) and say, "How very strange." But when we return in our imagination to our own context, it may be our world and not that of Francis which seems strange. Through the medium of the story and the imagination of the reader, the past becomes present. We are invited to pick up the plotline with our lives and live out in our own context this open-ended story that stretches from century to century, from moment to moment.

The story of Francis not only interprets our contemporary reality, but it can also empower us to construct reality in a distinctly Franciscan way. We are called not to imitate Francis slavishly or to agree to a doctrinal platform, but to become active participants in an open-ended story. Our participation in that story will require a fresh and creative appropriation of it in new and ever-changing circumstances. We can only do what we can imagine, and the stories of Francis enable us to imagine new ways of living out the gospel of Jesus Christ.

We acknowledge our indebtedness to the Franciscan family for preserving and retelling the story of Francis down through the ages. Thomas of Celano, an early contemporary of Francis, will be cited as a major source, as will Bonaventure, who wrote his version of the Francis story some forty years after the death of Francis. We also wish to acknowledge two Franciscans and a veteran journalist whose more contemporary interpretations have greatly influenced our thinking. These are Eloi Leclerc, the European author of *The Canticle of Creatures: Symbols of Union*; Leonardo Boff, the Brazilian author of *Saint Francis: A Model for Human Liberation;* and Paul Moses, author of *The Saint and the Sultan.* Moses's reading of Francis's story was particularly revealing as we began to revise the book. His study of Francis's visit to the Sultan, his reflections on Francis as a peacemaker, and his perspective on the church politics that influenced the biographies of both Thomas of Celano and Bonaventure were new and challenging insights that had an impact on our revisions.

Process of the Book

The method of this book assumes that several elements working together in a flowing, interactive, and dynamic fashion are essential to long-lasting social transformation grounded in biblical faith. These elements include theological reflection, scriptural study, social analysis, reflection on personal history and experience, and active response. Each element depends upon the others for its full meaning. Every chapter in the book is composed of these elements and of a specific Franciscan narrative around which the aforementioned elements revolve. In this way we sought to ground this inquiry into contemporary discipleship in the "circle of praxis," an ongoing process of reflection on social reality and action that aims to transform that reality. This term was first used by liberation theologians to describe a recurring cycle involving experience, social analysis, planning, and action.

In this introductory discussion of narrative we have mentioned the elements of scripture study, theological reflection, personal cultural history, and Franciscan narrative. A few words might be useful regarding the remaining two elements, social analysis and action response.

Social analysis (signs of our time): We have said that we best imitate Francis by following Jesus in a creative and fresh appropriation of the story of Francis for our own context. Our context is infinitely complex, changing with tremendous speed, and, of course, multifaceted. It is political, economic, social, local, international, psychological, ecological, and spiritual. Some would say that the particular circumstances of our day constitute a *kairos* moment, a moment pregnant with crisis, opportunity, and a call to discipleship. In order to follow Jesus by following Francis, we must dig into and seek to understand this complex contemporary context. We must not shy away—as so many of us are prone to do—from the quest to unravel the seemingly overwhelming social realities of our day. Without so doing, we cannot creatively appropriate the gospel story for our times as Francis did for his.

Action response (invitation to respond): It is far too easy and too common to avoid allowing our newly gained insight to change the way in which we live. The action-response component is meant to challenge us to live a deeper understanding of discipleship discovered in renewed reflection on the Franciscan tradition.

Finally, we hope and intend that this book will be used primarily by people reflecting on it together with other people with whom they share a significant level of trust, caring, and accountability. This intent rests upon our belief that the community of believers is an essential part of Christian discipleship—and upon our own experiences, which have taught us that transformative learning happens best in the context of community.

A Few Comments on an Ecumenical Experiment

Across wide denominational lines people of faith are recognizing with increasing clarity that we are in a global crisis that demands a new response from the church. It is not a time for clinging to our separateness as denominations; nor is this a time to abandon our traditions. We as Christians are being called to go more deeply into our common tradition to return to our roots. This is the meaning of *radical*—a going to the roots. To reclaim our tradition, our history, our story as gospel people is to be radical. To reclaim our roots is also to create a new basis for ecumenicity, a foundation of unity that is far greater than the historical differences that separate the different bodies of the church universal.

The authors of this volume hope that this is evident in the work to follow. We are very different—two Catholics, two Protestants; two men and two women; two ordained and two lay people. And yet herein was the tremendous gift of our time together as we gathered originally for a period of months to reflect on the story of Francis, the gospel story, and our own stories. The same gift was present when we reconvened twenty years later with new stories and new insights to revise the book.

Perhaps you can imagine some of the conversation at late-night or early morning gatherings as the four of us wrestled with, for example, the idea of sainthood itself. Many in the Catholic community are all too familiar with the lives of the saints because they were exhorted to strive to imitate these examples of perfection. Saints were admirable, perhaps, but in no way imitable. The residue of such devotion to the saints was, for many Roman Catholics, a pervasive sense of guilt and failure. The Protestant community, we found, has a different problem. Eager to purify the church of what it saw to be the excesses of hagiography, or what had become in the view of some the worship of saints, Protestants rejected outright a rich tradition of individuals and communities in the history of the church. Yet this tradition of the saints, though predating the Reformation, is "protestant" in the deepest sense of the word: it embodies a prophetic alternative to the status quo that calls the church to reform.

For Protestant and Catholic alike, the lives of the saints can model liberating alternatives. This cloud of witnesses has the power to reform and transform the church by calling each of us to our own vocation to sainthood, to transformed lives. In the volume to follow we have sought to place ourselves in dialogue with one of those saints, Francis of Assisi, to learn how he and his community responded creatively to the struggles faced in their own historical moment.

Our intent in these reflections is not really to call others to imitate Francis. In fact, we best imitate Francis by following Jesus in a creative appropriation of the gospel story for our own context. Francis's consuming goal was to follow Jesus. In hearing the story of how the saint of Assisi sought to live out a radical discipleship, we find new perspectives on how to live out our own call to be followers of Jesus. Our hope is to inspire spiritual, political, and historical reflection and meditation on the life of Francis; to dialogue with his life and witness; and to reflect deeply on the questions that these raise. Jesus first introduced us to the ideas of Francis. But Francis can reintroduce us to Jesus in a radical way. This story is then offered to all, not just those in Franciscan or Catholic communities, but to all Christians in the universal church who are trying to follow Jesus at a time of historical crisis.

Canticle of Creation

Most High, all-powerful, all good Lord!
All praise is yours, all glory, all honor and
    blessing.
To You alone, Most High, do they belong.
All praise be yours, my Lord, through all that
    you have made,

And first my Lord, Brother Sun,
Who brings the day, and light You give us
    through him.
How beautiful is he, how radiant in all his
    splendor!
Of You, Most High, he bears the likeness.

All praise be yours, my Lord, through Sister
    Moon and Stars;
In the heavens you have made them bright and
    fair.

All praise be yours, my Lord, through Brothers
    Wind and Air,
And fair and stormy, all the weather's moods,
By which you cherish all that You have made.

All praise be yours, my Lord, through Sister
    Water,
So useful, lowly, precious and pure.

All praise be Yours, my Lord, through Brother
    Fire,
Through whom you brighten up the night.
How beautiful he is, how gay! Full of power
    and strength.

All praise be yours, my Lord, through Sister
    Earth, our mother,
Who feeds us in her sovereignty and produces
Various fruits and colored flowers and herbs.

All praise be yours, my Lord, through those
    who grant pardon
For love of You; through those who endure sick-
    ness and trial.
Happy those who endure in peace,
By you, Most High, they will be crowned.

All praise be yours, my Lord, through Sister
    Death,
From whose embrace no mortal can escape.
Woe to those who die in mortal sin.
Happy those she finds doing your will!
The second death can do no harm to there.

Praise and bless my Lord, and give thanks.
Serve God with great humility.

Prologue

Why After You, Francis?
Why After You?

*One day when St. Francis was coming back from the
woods, where he had been praying, and was at the edge of
the forest, Brother Masseo went to meet him, as he wanted
to find out how humble he was, and he said to St. Francis,
half jokingly: "Why after you? Why after you? Why after
you?"*

*St. Francis replied, "What do you mean, Brother Mas-
seo?"*

*"I mean, why does all the world seem to be running after
you, and everyone seems to want to see you and hear you
and obey you? You are not a handsome man. You do not
have great learning or wisdom. You are not a nobleman. So
why is all the world running after you?" (Brown, 62–63)*

After Jesus himself, Francis of Assisi stands as the most popular and best-known figure in Christian history. Despite this, or
perhaps because of it, we choose to add yet another volume to
the already abundant material about him. Why?

Two inextricably related reasons motivate us. First, we are
convinced that the saint of Assisi has a crucial message for us:
for today's non-poor, the privileged of the world, the affluent of
the early twenty-first century.

We address this book primarily to the non-poor who wish to understand the meaning of Christian commitment in an impoverished world. Modern life suffers from, and paradoxically foments, isolation, injustice, violence, greed, and alienation from friendship and community. We believe that the values and spirituality of Francis contain a great lesson for contemporary privileged societies. Our offering, then, is an exploration of the outrageousness of the Poverello who found joy and fulfillment in walking at the margins of acceptable society.

Yet his message, surprisingly, does not condemn us; rather, it invites us to walk a similar journey—a pathway that moves toward the New Creation (see Isa 65:17–25). Moreover, despite our geographical, historical, psychological, and even spiritual distance from him, Francis's message contains a relevance and modernity to which his entire popularity gives testimony. His message, calling to us from the past, points to the joy, the pain, and, yes, the hilarity of constant conversion. We believe that Francis's spirituality embodies a convergence of mysticism, liberation theology, and prophetic evangelism that speak loudly to those contemporary Christians who long to do something about inequity and poverty, about consuming consumerism and driven emptiness.

The second reason for this book complements the first: it can be described as Francis's discomfort factor. Like it or not, the life of this popular Christian saint presents us with startling paradoxes. An enormously free and spontaneous person, he nevertheless adhered faithfully to the institutional church; a fully alive human being, he embraced suffering; a true lover, he chose celibacy; born into relative affluence, he practiced a literal poverty. These and so many other aspects of Francis's life inevitably give us pause to ponder today; that is, unless we have the questionable ability to ignore these unsettling aspects of his personality and deal only with the sentimental and "popular" sides of this complex man—his joy, love for nature, and familiarity with animals. As honest persons we need to delve into the real, flesh-and-blood, historical Francis. Otherwise we risk missing something of essence underlying his more familiar traits. Therefore we attempt here to present Francis to readers in the global North in as complete a fashion as possible, incorporating into our revised version a deeper exploration of his visit to the Sultan and his radical transformation from soldier to peacemaker.

These reasons for yet another book about Francis of Assisi require at least a brief look at his life in its historical framework. It is impossible to understand this person—as it is impossible to understand any human being—without at least a rudimentary grasp of the world that he inhabited.

The end of the twelfth and the beginning of the thirteenth centuries, when Francis lived, have been described as a time of awakening in Europe. The so-called Dark Ages had given way to the Middle Ages. The next hundred years would witness the beginning of the Renaissance, the rebirth of European culture and the real beginning of modern times. Among the many signs that this awakening was taking place was that Western Europe was becoming an area of surplus population, surplus productivity, and accelerated economic development. In addition, or as a consequence, the breakdown of the feudal system was leading to the emergence of city-states and a middle class. Feudalism would last a couple more centuries, but the seeds of its destruction had been sown, and this, together with rising affluence, constituted the central historical reality in the life of St. Francis.

Where wealth abounds, can poverty be absent? The underside of new economic realities was a growing impoverishment of the masses. For in this incipient capitalistic system, as in its more sophisticated expressions, some people gained while many suffered. Francis saw this phenomenon and reacted to it vigorously.

The Catholic Church at that time was at the height of its power and influence. This was not an unmitigated good. Not two hundred years later—a very short time in the two-thousand-year history of the Roman communion—Pope Alexander VI would epitomize the corruption that overtook the church. And three hundred years after Francis, the Protestant Reformation would sweep across Europe.

Within this historical and geographical reality one can capsulize Francis's life with relative ease. Born in 1182, he was the son of a very successful cloth merchant, Pietro Bernardone, and a French woman, Lady Pica. At age twenty, after a comfortable and somewhat frivolous youth at the head of a group called Merrymakers, the future saint marched off to one of the numerous wars then being fought between Italy's city-states. Imprisonment, sickness, and consequent disillusionment followed quickly, and Francis began to sense a different call. In dreams he heard himself called to another kind of chivalry—that of following "the great King." Tired of military adventurism and probably traumatized by the brutality of war, the young Francis began to divest himself of his considerable material possessions, thereby incurring his father's displeasure. A life-changing break with Don Pietro came in front of Assisi's good bishop when Francis literally removed the clothes given him by his father and uttered the startling statement: "From now on, I can walk naked before the Lord, no longer saying 'my father, Pietro Bernardino,' but 'Our Father who art in Heaven.'"

Thenceforth Francis followed Jesus according to his understanding of what that meant. First, he thought that the call he heard to "rebuild my church" referred to the broken-down chapels around Assisi. The youth collected stones and other materials to refurbish these buildings. Gradually, as others joined him, he came to realize that his was a deeper and further-reaching vocation. The growing brotherhood (and, thanks to Clare, the sisterhood) helped Francis see that God had chosen him to inspire a great movement of renewal in the church. The rest of his life was lived following that ideal.

Some highlights of the years following Francis's dramatic conversion include his vision and nurturing of community, his mission of peace to the Sultan, and his deep friendships, especially with Clare. These and other events in Francis's life point to years of intense activity combined with an all-abiding sense of God's presence.

Francis was by all accounts passionate, impulsive, extroverted, fun-loving, and poetic. He may well also have been moody, given to introspection, mystical, demanding, and at times fearful. He was Italian, after all, possessed of the substantial gifts as well as the wonderful paradoxes of that singular people.

During the final period of his life Francis wrote the Canticle of Creation, perhaps the best known of his recorded words. It summed up the saint's abiding and integrating sense of God and God's presence in all that exists. Two years before his death Francis received the wounds of the Crucified in his hands, feet, and side. This gift of God sealed his closeness to the Savior and prepared him for his final days on earth. These were marked by great suffering as well as enormous joy. Francis of Assisi died on October 3, 1226, at age forty-four.

The "distant mirror" held up to our times and our struggles leads us to confront the contradictions we face in our world today with a hope born of grace alone. Francis offers us the possibility of true joy, freedom, and love extending far beyond the boundaries of the familiar and based on an experience of God's mercy. Francis challenges us, not by avoiding human suffering and the negative side of human existence, but by embracing them.

Thus in coming to know Francis as we wrote this book, we increasingly encountered him as a prime example of "God's Fool." From the moment he got down from his horse and forced himself to embrace a leper at the beginning of his conversion, Francis saw the world in all its glorious absurdity—and acted on what he saw. He stood naked before his father and other Assisians in the bishop's courtyard; he sang to the birds; he lived the rest of his life at the margins of society. The biblical and theological notion of "the Fool" has thus enlivened these pages and is perhaps the one great lesson we, the authors, take from this labor. We shall return to it throughout the book and in our epilogue.

Finally, this walk with Francis, at a distance of eight centuries, is placed at the disposal of Christians in the global North. We offer it to all who are troubled by the poverty of affluence, by the insults to God's creation, by unrelenting violence, by demeaning human misery all around. We offer it to an ecumenical community that seeks to link faith with action as global citizens. To you, dear brothers and sisters, members of the household of faith in Jesus the Christ, we offer this modest attempt, as we strive together to move beyond the limitations imposed by fear, attachment to possessions, and weakness in our faith. Our guide in this common, enduring enterprise is the subject of this book, St. Francis of Assisi.

The Conversion of Francis

Encounter with the Marginalized

*And, raising his eyes toward his disciples, he
  said:*
*Blessed are you who are poor; for the kingdom
  of God is yours.*
*Blessed are you who are hungry now; for you
  will be satisfied.*
*Blessed are you who are now weeping; for you
  will laugh.*
*Blessed are you when people hate you, and
  when they exclude and insult you . . .*
Rejoice and leap for joy on that day!
Behold, your reward will be great in heaven.
  *For their ancestors treated the prophets
  in the same way. (Luke 6:20–23)*

FRANCIS'S STORY

All biographies of St. Francis point to his embrace of the
leper on the Umbrian plain as the crucial moment in his initial
conversion. Francis's encounter with the leper occurred very

early—before his break with his father. Its impact on him was unexpected and incalculable and, in many ways, set the tone for the rest of his life and mission, as well as for the lives and mission of his followers.

Lacking our understanding of Hansen's disease as curable, societies in Francis's day (as in Jesus's day) excluded people with leprosy from normal social and economic interactions. Though they were cared for separately, lepers in reality joined beggars and other social outcasts who lived on the margins of societies. In our times lepers are not often ostracized, but many others are—by custom, religious practice, racism, greed, sexism, intolerance, and systemic and structural injustice.

Leonardo Boff writes about the "privilege of the poor in the conversion process of Francis" (Boff 1984/2006, 68). Through those who were marginalized—the lepers and the very poor—the Spirit led Francis into the mystery of the cross. This encounter with the Crucified One clarified and deepened Francis's ability to see others in his own society who also were hanging on the cross.

According to biographer Johannes Jörgensen, lepers occupied a special place among the sick and the poor during the Middle Ages. They were, in fact, looked upon as an image of the Redeemer himself and were therefore the object of pious ministry. In the thirteenth century there were perhaps nineteen thousand homes for the care of lepers, one of which, near Assisi, was frequently passed by the young Francis. Yet, in spite of the care they were given, lepers were repulsed by the rest of society; they were severely restricted by laws that isolated them from all but the religiously motivated caretakers. Jörgensen writes of Francis's reaction:

> *The [leper] hospital lay midway between Assisi and Portiuncula. . . . On his walks in that place, Francis now and then passed by the hospital, but the mere sight of it had filled him with horror. He would not even give alms to a leper unless someone else would take it for him. Especially*

when the wind blew from the hospital, and the weak, nau-
seating odor, peculiar to the leper, came across the road,
he would hurry past with averted face and fingers in his
nostrils.

It was in this that he felt his greatest weakness, and in it
he was to win his greatest victory.

For one day, as he was as usual calling upon God, it
happened that the answer came. And the answer was this:
"Francis! Everything which you have loved and desired
in the flesh, it is your duty to despise and hate, if you wish
to know my will. And when you have begun thus, all that
which now seems to you sweet and lovely will become
intolerable and bitter, but all which you used to avoid will
turn itself to great sweetness and exceeding joy."

These were the words, which . . . showed him the way
he was to follow. He certainly pondered over these words
in his lonely rides over the Umbrian plain and, just as he
one day woke out of a reverie, he found the horse making
a sudden movement, and saw on the road before him, only
a few steps distant, a leper, in his familiar uniform.

Francis started, and even his horse shared in the move-
ment, and his first impulse was to turn and flee as fast as he
could. But there were the words he had heard within him-
self, so clearly before him—"what you used to abhor shall
be to you joy and sweetness." . . . And what had he hated
more than the lepers? Here was the time to take the Lord
at His word—to show his good will. . . . And with a mighty
victory over himself, Francis sprang from his horse, ap-
proached the leper, from whose deformed countenance the
awful odor of corruption issued forth, placed his alms in the
outstretched wasted hand—bent down quickly and kissed
the fingers of the sick man, covered with the awful disease,
whilst his system was nauseated with the action. . . .

When he again sat upon his horse, he hardly knew how
he had got there. He was overcome by excitement, his heart

beat, he knew not whither he rode. But the Lord had kept his word. Sweetness, happiness, and joy streamed into his soul—flowed and kept flowing, although his soul seemed full and more full—like the clear stream which, filling an earthen vessel, keeps on pouring and flows over its rim, with an ever clearer, purer stream. . . .

The next day, Francis voluntarily wandered down the road he had hitherto always avoided. . . . And when he reached the gate [to the leprosarium], he knocked, and when it was opened to him he entered. From all the cells the sick came swarming out—came with their half-destroyed faces, blind inflamed eyes, with club feet, with swollen, corrupted arms and fingerless hands. And all this dreadful crowd gathered around the young merchant, and the odor from their unclean swellings was so strong that Francis against his will for a moment had to hold his breath to save himself from sickness. But he soon recovered control of himself, he drew out the well-filled purse he had brought with him, and began to deal out his alms. And on every one of the dreadful hands that were reached out to take his gifts he imprinted a kiss, as he had done the day before. (Jörgensen, 38–39)

As a result of this experience of coming so close to the most despised, Francis was filled with wonder and joy. Jesus's beatitudes (Luke 6:20–23) must have been very much on his mind in this regard. "Blessed are you poor, yours is the kingdom of heaven." The significance of this scripture, which had been in the collective Christian memory since the time of Jesus, began to emerge, enfleshed and vibrant, for Francis.

Thereafter, he sought contact at the margins time and time again, gradually allowing his own process of conversion to be informed by the experience of encounter with poor people. At first he had despised the thought of touching the abhorred leper, but now the invitation to reconciliation was irresistible. Francis's deeply entrenched habit of pushing the leper to the edges of his space, as far away from him physically and emotionally as possible, was forever broken.

For Francis, the order of things was turned upside down, just as it had been for the apostles, whose experience of Jesus so often drew them into the mystery of the cross. Jesus, whom they followed and called friend, embraced, mingled with, touched, loved, cured, and broke bread with the outcasts, the marginal, the unclean of his day. The lives of the poor or rejected ones were and are intrinsically bound up with the journey of Jesus. "Blessed are the poor," indeed! Consistently and deliberately chosen encounters on the periphery of accepted society were woven into the fabric of who Jesus became. In a social structure shaped by exclusion of the leprous, the ritually unclean, the "non-chosen," the women, the possessed, tax collectors, sinners—Jesus embraced them all, both individually and as social groups. In fact, Jesus's very identity was as one who proclaimed the good news to the poor, who announced the inbreaking of the reign of God, and who lived the announcement by being at the side of the poor himself.

Encounter with Jesus in the Poor

In Francis's new upside-down order, his encounter with the leper was indeed an encounter with this Jesus in a person who was marginalized. The story of the leper symbolizes Francis's journey across a tremendous psychological and emotional barrier. Once he was able to transcend that dreaded barrier, he seemed to be able to move beyond and allow himself to be open to the "other" whom he had previously imagined to be so awful. It allowed him to move forward in leaps and bounds on his own journey, and to surmount the barriers that separate the clean from the unclean, the desirable from the undesirable, the haves from the have-nots. Once he was given the grace to do that, everything was changed for him. As Francis embraced a vivid example of human misery, he tasted great joy; the sweetness he experienced revealed God's presence pervading his meeting with the outcast. *Sweetness,* the very word Francis had used earlier to describe his profoundly ecstatic experience of God, is now used by him to describe the experience of knowing a leper.

Following Francis, Following Jesus

In *A Theology of Liberation* Gustavo Gutiérrez writes about the evolution of our encounters with God. Moving from the mountaintop to the ark of the covenant to the Temple to the neighbor, the Jewish and Christian traditions have called us to celebrate the sacrament of the "other," especially the most marginal, as blessed location of the indwelling Spirit.

> *God's temple is human history; the "sacred" transcends the narrow limits of the places of worship. We find the Lord in our encounters with [others], especially the poor, the marginated, the exploited ones. An act of love toward them is an act of love toward God. This is why Yves Congar speaks of the "sacrament of our neighbor," who as a visible reality reveals to us and allows us to welcome the Lord. (Gutiérrez, 155)*

Blessed Are You Who Weep Now . . .

Encountering the impoverished, walking for a while in the world of the marginalized, and being with the have-nots of our world is a necessary aspect of the discipleship journey. Our vision thereafter is shaped by this encounter. We realize, and never forget, the privileged perspective of impoverished people who see reality with a clarity of vision that we may never achieve. Our souls are touched by the encounter as well, and sorrow over the pain and injustice of impoverishment and marginalization fills the crevices of our being. The painful side of the paradox—the misery of poverty—presents itself once again.

> Look, O Lord, upon my distress:
>   All within me is in ferment. . . .
> Give heed to my groaning;
>   There is no one to console me. (Lam 1:20–21)

Deep mourning over the social conditions that make people poor may be the first step we non-poor can take to internalize the beatitudes: "Blessed are you who are now weeping; you shall laugh." Mourning implies a terrible sense of loss, of regret, an acknowledgment of the real, and a feeling of pain in the face of that reality. Weeping and mourning emerge from our affective side and are profoundly healthy emotions for those of us who are more privileged, who will never fully share the lot of those who are impoverished by the system that creates our wealth, but who at least can weep over the tragedy of human suffering. Emotions help describe us as whole people and, if joined with righteous indignation at the injustices that cause marginalization, can lead us toward a relinquishment of the power and privilege that maintain injustice, and toward a solidarity with those who are poor in their claim on justice.

The grief-stricken wailing of Lamentations was written in the days of the prophet Jeremiah, the sixth century BCE, a turning point in the story of the people of Israel and an unprecedented time of crisis for a people who failed to hear the prophetic call to social transformation. The Temple was destroyed and its ritual interrupted; leading citizens were taken into exile; and the disintegration of society resulted in captivity that separated the people from the land that carried their communal identity.

Our times, too, are times of crisis. Our society faces escalating social and moral disintegration, a devastating captivity to ways of life that perpetrate injustice, marginalization, and extreme poverty of body and soul. The prophetic call of Jeremiah echoes around us, and we too are wont to ignore it. Exile seems inevitable, and its parameters are beginning to emerge: massive indebtedness (both public and private); dehumanizing poverty; lack of meaningful work; rampant violence (in structures, streets, and even our homes); isolation from community; loss of roots; emptiness in place of meaningful existence; ecological crises; and so on.

The book of Lamentations moves from confession of sin through profound grief to strong faith in the constancy of Yahweh's love and fidelity. We, too, can move from confession of sin and deep mourning through righteous anger toward a hope-filled embrace of a better, more life-giving Way.

The Paradox of Joy

In the context of our mourning, however, the joy described by Francis in his encounter with the leper presents us with a disturbing paradox. In itself, contact with poor people does not generate the sort of sweetness that Francis claims—at least not at first. Dehumanizing poverty and marginalization are ugly blights upon the contours of creation. Our encounter with those who are crucified and who are struggling for liberation brings us, as it brought Francis, face to face with excruciating pain and offers much food for reflection. Indeed, to walk with people who are poor, to share their lives and struggles, to accompany the "least" of our brothers and sisters in the painful places they inhabit can and must occasion anger, rage, and the desire to change the way things are. Paradoxically, this encounter with those suffering on the margins can also occasion amazing joy. The claim of the Gospel ("Yours is the reign of God. . . . You shall laugh!") and of St. Francis that one can find God and profound pleasures of the soul in meeting the poor is hard to believe, especially for the non-poor.

Initially, perhaps, we can only accept this on faith, but slowly we will experience it, sometimes in contrast with the barrenness of affluence, as we summon the courage, not to make poverty look better, but to step into the suffering of the poor ones as Francis did. There, in the place of empty consumerism, it is possible to encounter life-giving values. In the place of individualism we can find common struggle; in the places of greed we frequently see generosity beyond belief. Here we do have a paradox. Poverty is ugly and dehumanizing; it is an evil that must be eliminated. Yet, in encountering impoverished people, we often discover beauty and graced humanity. Indeed, in encountering the poor ones of our world, we often find God.

Accompaniment: The Joy of the Gospel

Pope Francis captured this paradox in *The Joy of the Gospel (Evangelii gaudium)*. Less than a year after being elected, Francis wrote:

> *This entails appreciating the poor in their goodness, in their experience of life, in their culture, and in their ways of living the faith. True love is always contemplative, and permits us to serve the other not out of necessity or vanity, but rather because he or she is beautiful above and beyond mere appearances: "The love by which we find the other pleasing leads us to offer him something freely." The poor person, when loved, "is esteemed as of great value," and this is what makes the authentic option for the poor differ from any other ideology, from any attempt to exploit the poor for one's own personal or political interest. (no. 199)*

Each of us, no doubt, can recall moments of grace-filled interaction that have called us beyond what we are toward what we can be, both as individuals and as communities of faith. For many, these moments of grace have taken place in encounters like that of Francis with the leper. Conversion, and the resultant freedom of the spirit, even joy, have often begun in an encounter with someone living on the margins: with homeless people or refugees in our own communities; with those who are impoverished or sick with AIDS on the other side of the world; with survivors of torture or war; with families who have lost their land, their mountains, their water, their health to a greedy world.

Years ago, during the worst of the wars in Central America, many US Americans experienced this kind of dialogue with communities in El Salvador, Guatemala, or Nicaragua. Some of us, for example, accompanied displaced *campesino* families back to their land in El Salvador after years of war. Tired of living dependent lives in refugee camps, the people had decided to go home. It was time to return to cultivate their land, to reclaim their roots, to enflesh values of life in the midst of death and violence, and internationals were invited to accompany them, providing by our presence a modicum of protection, as they were going back to their villages in the midst of a war in which they were clearly targets.

On the way to the *campo* we laughed together and prayed together, we held the children together, hauled debris from the bombed-out shells of the village together, and broke bread in Eucharist together. We stood together when the army came, and we wept as the soldiers separated us.

It was the sort of time when dialogue could lead to an understanding of the spirit of a people—a time to hear another's language and see another's culture in a new way and to understand better the hopes and fears of very poor and very courageous people living in the most difficult of circumstances. What we learned dramatically turned our non-poor perceptions of the world upside down, as the encounter with the leper turned Francis's world upside down: "Blessed are the poor."

The Role of the Non-Poor

Francis's embrace of the leper was both a personal leap of faith and, at the same time, a social statement akin to the sort of social statement that paved Jesus's way to the cross. What social statements are we called to make in the face of the poverty of our own world? In other words, what is the role of the non-poor in relation to the liberation journeys of those who are impoverished and marginalized, not only in Latin America, but in our own country and in other parts of the world? How do we respond to the fear and rage we often feel when faced with poverty? How do we respond to the grace and goodness we encounter? How do we learn to move from pity to love, from charity to justice, from the one poor person to the many? How do we discern the causes of poverty and identify ways to challenge and overcome exploitative structures? What is our responsibility in the creation of a more just and peaceful world?

Our response might best be summed up by the word *accompaniment:* to deviate from other pathways for a while (and then forever), to walk together with those on the margins, to be with them, to let go. Accompaniment is an idea so radical and difficult for us to comprehend that its power for mutual healing and significance reveal themselves to our Euro-western and northern minds only slowly and with great difficulty. Through this encounter with Christ at the margins, we, who with Francis once saw the poor only as the "other," the feared one, the object of dread, then pity, then charity, can, as individuals and societies, experience a profound, ongoing, Spirit-led conversion of heart, soul, and mind. Slowly, as marginalized people allow us to walk with them, our center of gravity moves outside of ourselves and we find ourselves suddenly dancing with the Poverello and his despised friends in unknown places and with great joy.

It is a way of life well known to Francis—and to the Oscar Romeros, Ita Fords, and Dorothy Days among us, who probed the depths of incarnation, crucifixion, and resurrection, and who knew that their soul would never be the same. It is a way of life that makes sense out of Jesus's embrace of and friendship with the outcast.

It is an idea that at first glimpse seems utterly simple but, when tried, stretches the limits of our theological understanding and our spirituality, challenges our worldview, pushes us toward horizons we never thought we could reach, and turns upside down the question of our role in the creation of a more just and peaceful world.

Consider again the Sermon on the Mount:

> Blessed are you poor; yours is the Reign of God.
> Blessed are you who are hungry now; you shall
>   be satisfied.
> Blessed are you who weep now; you shall laugh.
> Blessed are you when people hate you, drive you
>   out, abuse you. . . .
> your reward with be great. (Luke 6:20–23)

Do we dare to believe it? Do we dare to believe that poor and hungry people will be satisfied and that those who are weeping will laugh? Do we dare to believe that in these times God incarnate is suffering crucifixion and redeeming us still? Witness the faith of so many exploited and impoverished communities! See how often they love one another back to life—see how they struggle together to bring about the Reign of God, the New Creation, beginning with the basic necessities of life—potable water, education, health care, and so forth. Can we allow the grace of their challenging embrace to permeate our lives?

The invitation to accompaniment is a fragile invitation into the heart of the Christian faith—an invitation to witness the Spirit present in the suffering, struggles, and fidelity of poor people today. At some times the invitation is to an individual—a "stranger" inserted into the reality of a marginal world. In other situations, as in El Salvador, Haiti, South Africa, and Palestine, the invitation has been extended to the international community in general to experience concretely the painful results of injustice and poverty. This welcoming is a real and specific gesture of reconciliation. In the world today the lives of marginalized people in El Salvador, Mexico, Bangladesh, Cambodia, Afghanistan, Iraq, the D.R. Congo, and the cities and rural areas of our own country as well, are inextricably linked to our own—too often through our systems and structures, even our values, that oppress them.

It is incredible, therefore, that we are even occasionally invited into their embrace as they seek a more humane existence. It is a remarkable opportunity—a gift of great courage from impoverished people of this world to the non-poor.

We are invited to move step by step from our positions of privilege into greater solidarity with poor people and with Christ, who is incarnate on the margins of society. But our lifetime journey as non-poor must move beyond solidarity with the struggles of the marginalized, for those who are not poor, too, are children of God, called to be subjects of our own stories. As a class we also are necessary participants in the unique New Creation tasks given to us. As we accompany marginalized people—those deemed disposable by our society today—physically or politically, we experience the truth that we are also embraced and accompanied by them. As we struggle to find God in their land (the hovels and barrios, favelas, slums, and tenements so alien to many of us), as we struggle for the liberation of our cultural soul (so often captive to consumerism, to the media, to Wall Street or Madison Avenue, to cell phones, to the rat race of superficial living), we learn that they are the "beloveds" of this world who are drinking from the Cup of the One who accompanied us all. Their suffering and their efforts to claim a more human existence are one with the suffering of Jesus and with his announcement of the inbreaking reign of God. The lives of these marginal ones continue the crucifixion and promise resurrection. As a redemptive presence in our broken world, those who are poor accompany us.

Gift to the Non-Poor

As we are accompanied, everything changes. Common strug-gle begins to replace destructive individualism; generosity and concern for the other overcome individual and collective greed. Prayer, sacrament, community, and images of God are all trans-formed. Prayer becomes prophetic and, as Walter Brueggemann says, "impolite." Eucharist is nourishment for the long haul, a deep source of consolation and joy, and a profound challenge always to share the bread of hunger. Reconciliation is deep and gratifying, grounded in the most painful memories born from a dialogue of the heart—a dialogue about poverty and human suffering, about isolation, neglect, and violence—but clearly a dialogue leading toward new ways of being brother and sister in a broken world. Community—peoples in solidarity on their journey/our journey to liberation—becomes an essential element of life, a supportive, challenging, and life-giving element. Images of God are profoundly incarnational, drawn from the encounter with suffering, struggling humanity.

Francis's moment with the leper, then, has become a paradigm for understanding Francis. It was a grace-filled moment for him, a time of crisis, a *kairos*. We reflect on it because it explains so much about him. Francis always pointed to lepers and to the "dwelling place of lepers" as places where Franciscans should be. Francis's encounter with the leper was a moment of self-definition, self-revelation, and conversion. Our encounters at the margins of society can be a means of understanding ourselves as well—a grace-filled *kairos* for us as individuals and as a society.

Pope Francis has repeatedly articulated a similar message and given powerful witness to it by his own way of life, which is deliberately and repeatedly in contact with those who are margin-alized in our times: refugees, prisoners, those who are suffering physically or impoverished. "We need to touch the wounds of Jesus," he said at mass at Casa Santa Marta. "We must caress the wounds of Jesus; we need to bind the wounds of Jesus with tenderness, we have to kiss the wounds of Jesus, and this literally. Just think of what happened to St. Francis, when he embraced the leper? The same thing that happened to Thomas: his life changed. To touch the living God" (Pope Francis, July 3, 2013).

OUR STORIES

Reflect on your own relationship to people who are poor or marginalized. Go back into your memory and recall your earliest conscious experience with people you considered poor or outcast. If you were poor as a child, recall when you first realized it. In either case:

• What did you think? What did you feel? What did you do?

• How did the experience influence your subsequent impressions of poor people?

• What are the images, characteristics, and assumptions about poor people that you absorbed as you grew up?

• Imagine someone poor visiting your home. How would you feel? Imagine someone with much more money, social status, or education than you have visiting your home. How would you feel?

SIGNS OF OUR TIMES

We know that today the "leper," or outcast, is not only a single individual whom we might encounter as we go out from familiar to new realities. Today the outcast is thousands of homeless people who huddle in subway stations or on steam grates in our cities. The outcast is the battered woman who seeks shelter from an impossible domestic situation. The outcast is the deinstitutionalized mental patient walking the streets in a daze. The outcast is a malnourished child—in Alabama or Bangladesh,

Haiti or Uganda, Cambodia or New York—who could be fed with the excess of our tables. The outcast is a young person in an impoverished country who will never have a decent quality of life because of preventable disease, poor education, overcrowded job markets, and unjust wages.

The outcasts of today, tragically, are the majority of the earth's population, the billions who live in poverty and the countless others who are continually pushed to the periphery of our societies. In our own time we have unprecedented access to information about the breadth and depth of marginalization. With modern communications technologies, we cannot *not* know that millions of men, women, and children in the United States and around the world are homeless; that millions of children in the United States live below the poverty line; that hundreds of millions of adults in the world are illiterate; that deep, endemic poverty robs a large percentage of the global population of any chance at a dignified life.

We cannot help hearing the stories and statistics about people living in poverty, but too often we hear only part of the story. Like Francis's early perceptions of the lepers, we see impoverished people as objects of pity or blame. We pull back from the suffering and miss the gift of relationships that are so often life-giving.

> *The times talk to us of so much poverty in the world and this is a scandal. Poverty in the world is a scandal. In a world where there is so much wealth, so many resources to feed everyone, it is unfathomable that there are so many hungry children, that there are so many children without an education, so many poor persons. Poverty today is a cry. (Pope Francis, meeting with students of Jesuit Schools, June 7, 2013)*

Do we ever explore the roots of poverty? Do we ever ask why? According to Joe Holland and Peter Henriot, in their classic book *Social Analysis: Linking Faith and Justice*, "Social analysis can be defined as the effort to obtain a more complete picture of a social situation by exploring its historical and structural relationships." Some questions to ponder in the light of the "signs of the times" described above:

• What are the statistics now for global poverty, childhood poverty in the United States, illiteracy worldwide and in the United States?

• Has the situation changed in recent years?

• What kinds of decisions have led to this situation or to recent changes in the poverty picture?

• Who has made and continues to make these decisions?

• Who has benefitted from these decisions? Who bears the burdens?

• Who can make decisions that could change the situation?

• How can you participate in this change?

INVITATION TO RESPOND

Having read of Francis's encounter with the leper and reflected on it in light of the beatitudes, we are called to respond with action. Like Jesus and Francis, we are commanded by God to "bring good news to the poor," and we are assured by the life of Jesus and the witness of Francis that we will find good news among the poor. But to do both, we must move to the margins where we can encounter impoverished people.

Draw a circle that defines your "familiar world." Write in it all those whose lives regularly intersect with your own. Write outside your circle those whose lives rarely touch yours. Begin with the following list, but add to it from your own experience:

immediate family
coworkers
neighbors
homeless people
refugees
people with AIDS
people of other racial groups than your own
people who are poor
those in prison
people with physical disabilities
the elderly
the mentally or emotionally ill

Note that in his encounter with the leper, Francis had to go out. He did not come upon the leper until he had moved toward him, however unconsciously or unknowingly.

Have you felt a call to go out of your familiar world toward the "other," the stranger, the needy one? Think of a particular instance when you have experienced such an invitation.

Have you allowed yourself, even forced yourself literally, to move to another place in order to embrace a hurting world, to walk in the shoes of a suffering person, to understand those who are poor? How?

Let God lead you again and again to the outcast, whoever he or she might be. Let the experience be a reflective one, not a dutiful going among poor people, but a conscious and meditative move from the familiar to the world of hurt—perhaps in the very same soup kitchen or hospice that you have visited before. Allow the experience to challenge your assumptions about the margins and to push you toward an appropriate response.

2

Francis and Relinquishment

Ongoing Conversion

As he was setting out on a journey, a man ran up, knelt down before him, and asked him, "Good teacher, what must do to inherit eternal life?" . . . "You know the commandments: 'You shall not kill; you shall not commit adultery; you shall not steal; you shall not bear false witness; you shall not defraud; honor your father and your mother.'"

He . . . said to him, "Teacher, all of these I have observed from my youth." Jesus, looking at him, loved him and said to him, "You are lacking in one thing. Go, sell what you have, and give to [the] poor and you will have treasure in heaven; then come, follow me." At that statement his face fell, and he went away sad, for he had many possessions. Jesus looked around and said to his disciples, "How hard it is for those who have wealth to enter the kingdom of God!" The disciples were amazed at his words. (Mark 10:17–24)

FRANCIS'S STORY

Here we look at the moment in the life of Francis when he stripped himself naked in the courtyard of the cathedral, in front of his own family, the bishop, and the townspeople of Assisi.

By this time, Francis had experienced the transforming encounter with the leper. In Chapter 1 we reflected on that story, in which Francis is called to conversion in an encounter with impoverished people of his world. Soon after that Francis heard a voice telling him to "rebuild my church." He sold his father's goods and used the proceeds for the work of repairing a ruined chapel called San Damiano. Francis later went into hiding from his father but was found and imprisoned by the elder Bernardone. The conflict between father and son grew until it reached the breaking point described below. This was a decisive moment in Francis's conversion, when Francis took the leap of faith from his world into that of the marginalized through a radical relinquishment of status and security.

> *But when his father saw that he would not be able to recall Francis from the journey he had begun he was roused by all means to get back the money. The man of God had desired to offer it all to be spent on feeding the poor and on the repair of that church. But he, who loved not money, was not to be misled by any show of good that it might bring, and he who was not held back by any affection for it was in nowise disturbed at the loss of it. Therefore when the money was found which that greatest despiser of earthly things and that most eager searcher after heavenly riches had thrown aside into the dust of the window, the raging father's fury was somewhat appeased, and the thirst of his avarice in some sort allayed by the dew of discovery. Then he brought his son before the bishop of the city, so that by a formal renunciation of all his property in the bishop's presence he might give up all he had. And Francis not only did not refuse to do this, but, greatly, rejoicing, made haste with ready mind to perform what had been demanded of him.*
>
> *When brought before the bishop, Francis would brook no delay nor hesitation in anything: nay, without waiting*

*to be spoken to and without speaking he immediately put
off and cast aside all his garments and gave them back to
his father. Moreover he did not even keep his drawers but
stripped himself stark naked before all the bystanders. But
the bishop, observing his disposition, and greatly wonder-
ing at his fervor and steadfastness, arose forthwith, gathered him into his arms and covered him with the mantle
which he himself was wearing. He understood clearly that
"the counsel was of God," and perceived that the actions of
the man of God which he had witnessed enfolded a mystery.
Immediately therefore the bishop became his helper, and,
cherishing and encouraging him, he embraced him in the
bowels of charity. (Celano, First Life, nos. 14–15)*

Young Francis undoubtedly had been the topic of conversation around the hearths of Assisi for some time. Some must have
pitied him for what they saw to be the ravings of a madman. For
others his "antics" were a source of amusement or scorn. There
could be no doubt in anyone's mind that Francis had not been
the same since he returned from war with a deadly fever. But all
that had gone before would seem tame in comparison with this
moment. How fast did word spread around town that there was
some commotion down at the cathedral and that Francis was
at the center of it? How quickly would the townspeople gather
to witness this latest chapter in the ongoing scandal of the Bernardone family? What did they think when Francis dropped his
cloak? What emotions did they feel when he stood naked before
them all? Did anyone there in the courtyard, Francis included,
really understand the significance of what they saw? Do we?

The story of Francis stripping himself naked in the bishop's
courtyard conveys to us an essential moment in his conversion
process. As Francis stood there naked, completely vulnerable before the bishop, his family, and the people of Assisi, he divested
himself of much more than just his clothes and belongings. In

effect, he relinquished family identity and reputation and the security of his economic status. For Francis, this moment was a literal and symbolic letting go of his former life.

But we misunderstand the significance of this moment if we think that it was for Francis an end in itself. Francis did not pursue poverty as an ascetic ideal of self-denial. For Francis, this relinquishment was a practical means of relocating himself in relationship to people considered to be the lowest in the social order of his day. His break from his former life and status in Assisi was the prelude to his life and work among the marginalized people in the leper colony. Indeed, one cannot distinguish Francis's conversion experience from this journey into the lives of people on the margins of society: they are one and the same. His encounter with the leper, selling his father's goods, and stripping himself naked are all symbolic moments, steps in a conversion process. For Francis, it is relationship to people whom society has cast out that provides the genuine context for conversion.

To understand Francis and the role of relinquishment in our own faith journey, we must look beyond Francis to the gospel upon which he based his life and witness. Several gospel texts became absolutely normative for the life and practice of the early Franciscan community. The text from Mark cited above is one of those. Our purpose here is to continue our dialogue with Francis about the creative ways in which he followed Jesus in his own place and time. Hearing this story of how Francis lived his radical discipleship, we gain new perspectives on how to live our call to follow Jesus. Now we delve more deeply into this gospel story to see from another perspective how this word can become flesh in our lives and in our place and time.

An Encounter "Along the Way"

A man ran up and knelt before him, and asked him, "Good Teacher, what must I do to inherit eternal life?"

Immediately our story sets up an encounter between Jesus and an unnamed individual. The narrative begins to offer us clues about who this person is from the nature of their meeting. We notice that the man's approach to Jesus is formal and proper. He kneels before Jesus and calls him "Good Teacher" as a sign of respect. We suspect that this person has considerable social standing. The man asks about eternal life, a religious question that undoubtedly comes from the heart. Yet Jesus responds rather aloofly, "Why do you call me good?"

The Invitation to Discipleship

As if they were sparring with each other over the keeping of the Ten Commandments, Jesus deliberately inserts, "Do not defraud!" as a warning to the rich not to deprive workers of their just wage. Why, in speaking to a rich man, does Jesus interject into the traditional commandments this unprecedented admonition? The warning sears, as we realize the pervasiveness of wage theft in US society. How much wealth is made by denying workers the full value of their wages or benefits?

Here the story takes a remarkable turn. Jesus looks upon the individual and loves him. Jesus's initial aloofness yields to a genuine love for the individual standing before him. Recognizing the potential for discipleship, Jesus issues an invitation:

> *"You lack one thing; go, sell what you have, and give it to the poor, and you will have treasure in heaven; and come follow me." (Mark 10:21)*

At that, the sadness of the man betrays his inner struggle and, ultimately, his failure to respond to the invitation, at least at this initial point. As he turns away, we learn for the first time that he was indeed a rich person, "for he had great possessions."

Placed side by side the gospel text and the story of Francis are two analogous stories of rich men in a fundamental crisis that arises from the contradiction between the demands of discipleship and the possession of wealth in the presence of the poor. In response to this crisis, the one, genuinely seeking to move forward in his faith journey, is confronted by Jesus with this contradiction. Sadly, he turns away, unable to let go of his possessions and thus respond to the invitation. In the other story, the second rich man, from Assisi, takes a radical leap of faith; he relinquishes his hold on all worldly ties and possessions. Francis transposes himself from the world of his family and the emerging bourgeois class to the world of the most marginalized poor, whose plight worsened as their numbers steadily increased.

FOLLOWING FRANCIS, FOLLOWING JESUS

In our own time, does relinquishment play an essential role in our ongoing conversion as people of faith? This story from the biography of Francis has much to teach us, the non-poor, about the nature of our discipleship. We in the middle strata of the United States may not think of ourselves as rich or as financially well off, but if we look at the global reality and at abject poverty in our own nation, we know that we are indeed relatively rich, that the political and economic power wielded by the industrial Western nations makes us wealthy beyond comparison. In hearing this text we, as non-poor people of faith, come to a crossroad in our own discipleship journey.

At this juncture it is important for us to reflect on what made it possible for one wealthy person, and apparently impossible for the other, to respond affirmatively to the invitation to discipleship.

The Gospel: A Scandal and Stumbling Block to the Non-Poor?

If we are honest with ourselves, the gospel story of the rich man is most disturbing. The difficulty with this text for the church in the global north is rooted in the recognition that Jesus's call to discipleship and the man's inability to respond to that call challenge us directly. Non-poor people of faith have found this story very threatening because we have understood Jesus to mean that a contradiction exists between possessions and the demands of faith. Can we be who we are as middle-class people and still be faithful followers of Jesus? We must remember that Jesus looked upon the young man, loved him, and invited him to join his community. The non-poor are children of God and loved by Jesus. But when we open ourselves to this text, we are faced with the contradiction between authentic Christian faith and possessing more than we need while others lack the basic necessities of life.

The non-poor church's difficulty with the encounter between Jesus and the rich man is not surprising. Even the discipleship community around Jesus struggled to come to grips with the radical nature of what Jesus was proposing. As we move to the second section of the text, we see that Jesus is openly skeptical about the ability of the rich to respond to the call of discipleship. To underscore this point Jesus uses the metaphor of the camel and the eye of the needle, a bit of peasant humor that leaves no doubt about the conflict between wealth and discipleship. The disciples respond with astonishment, "Who then can be saved?" Our reaction as non-poor Christians echoes that of the disciples. Like them, the non-poor today have squirmed uncomfortably with this metaphor. We have softened its impact with interpretations that dilute the meaning of the story.

It is very difficult for non-poor Christians to "be with" this story for long without trying to find a theological loophole through which to escape. We tend to eliminate the contradiction by rewriting the metaphor to suit ourselves. We have taken this challenging story and the hundreds of other scriptural passages that address economic justice and put them in a jar on the shelf.

The easiest way to resolve this dilemma has been to ignore it and pretend that no contradiction is posed here. The contribution of Francis was to take the witness and words of the historical Jesus quite seriously and to strive to apply them radically to his own life. At the very least we as people of faith must remain in dialogue with this gospel story, even if it means being uncomfortable.

Continuing the dialogue, one might ask: What about us, the non-poor? Does this mean there is no place for us in the gospel story? The God of the poor does not reject us because we are non-poor or love us any less than those who are poor. Yet the oppression and impoverishment of our brothers and sisters demand a response from us. Christ beckons to us from the margins, in the human face of the impoverished, the "least of these," inviting each of us to join this struggle. If we, like Francis, are seeking to follow Jesus, we must begin to find ways to journey to the margins of society to encounter those on the "other side."

As we reflected in the previous chapter, the gospel calls us to the margins of society in order to bring about the conversion that is begun in our encounter with the impoverished people. The conversion of Francis was a profound change from seeing the leper as an abhorrent and despised non-person to seeing him as a brother in whom Christ dwells. In Francis's conversion of heart he began to feel and practice compassionate solidarity. In this chapter we reflect on the next stage of our response as we let go in order to enter more deeply into that conversion process. We are asked to move beyond our comfort zone, beyond the insulating boundaries of class and social status to places of greater risk, toward those on the margins.

As we share significant time with people on the bottom rungs of economic life, we quickly become aware of the tremendous abyss that separates us. It is rooted in racism, economic injustice, and fundamental social inequities. Our task as people who are not economically impoverished is to remove the obstacles created by society that prevent the liberation of those who are impoverished and marginalized. Our task is to walk with marginalized communities under their leadership to help create space for self-determination and freedom from oppression.

Our conversion may entail letting go of deeply held ways of seeing the world. As we emerge from the cocoon of middle-class existence and begin to see the world from the perspectives of people who are impoverished by the ways of life that provide our relative wealth, we discover a profoundly different reality. Our perspective is likely to be altered as we increasingly learn, with their help, to read reality from their perspective. Gradually we begin to understand our history and the forces that shape the present moment from the perspective of the "underside" of society. We see, for example, forces of white privilege and class privilege at play throughout the decades and the centuries, forces that have determined who today lives without the basic necessities of life. We see more clearly how it is that many people who work more than full time still do not earn enough to feed and shelter their families. This entails not only a profound shift in understanding but also a conversion of the way in which we live.

Relinquishment is much more than giving up material goods. It also means learning to recognize that the wealth of some is built on the impoverishment of others, and then how to relinquish our investment in those systems—how to expose and challenge them and build alternatives. Relinquishment, of course, takes multiple forms and is the work of people in community, not only of individuals. For many people it means supporting living-wage campaigns, even though higher prices might be the result. For others, it means withdrawing from global banking systems or investment firms and investing in local banks or socially responsible investment funds. Others choose to purchase food and other products that are produced without exploiting land or labor—even though those products may cost more—and then work to convince their church networks, local governments, and other institutions to do the same. Some believe that Jesus and Francis might be beckoning the United States as a nation to relinquish military dominance and invest in sustainable peace and inclusive security.

The emerging fossil-fuel divestment movement is yet another illustration. Increasingly, universities and faith communities are debating divestment from the fossil-fuel industry; many have taken that pledge because climate change presents one of the gravest threats to the lives and livelihoods of people already marginalized by poverty. Because climate change is caused overwhelmingly by the world's high-consuming people (who are disproportionally of European descent) and is most devastating to impoverished people (who are disproportionally people of color), climate change presents a new call to relinquishment—of our dependence on and overuse of fossil fuels. This too can take many directions.

Relinquishment as a call and a gift means giving up prestige and privilege, learning to listen and to accept criticism, and learning how to use our power differently and ultimately to share our power. At the very least our task as non-poor is to share the power available to us—our resources of wealth, education, influence, and access—with those who have been denied these things. This is not charity or noblesse oblige. It is a fundamental letting go to allow the very structures that benefit us to be transformed.

Our task as people of faith is to refashion, indeed, to re-create more equitable, open, and inclusive systems and structures, not just in the religious community but in the larger society. At first it may seem that we are being asked to work against our own interests and to our disadvantage. As structures and systems yield to change, we may experience sharing power as a loss of power or even a taste of powerlessness. But ultimately, as conditions of justice, equality, and self-determination begin to take shape in concrete ways, we will understand that what we have been about is the transformation of power from the power of domination to the power of compassionate solidarity. New possibilities will emerge for reconciliation, friendship, and a genuine empowerment grounded in community.

In the end we are faced with the awesome paradox of Christian faith that defies human definitions of power. In Jesus's apparent absolute powerlessness on the cross, indeed the complete self-abnegation of Jesus on the cross, God has radically overturned all human notions of power. Out of weakness comes strength; out of powerlessness comes power; out of death comes resurrection, life. This is part of the radical witness that Jesus, Paul, and Francis place before us: God's foolishness is wiser than human wisdom, and God's weakness stronger than human strength.

Losing Ourselves, We Find Ourselves

The way of relinquishment is the lifelong process of removing the obstacles to loving and just relationships with our neighbors on this earth and of moving toward more genuine community among all of God's children and indeed among all of earth's creatures and elements, the kind of sisterhood and brotherhood envisioned by Francis. As we help to remove the obstacles to the liberation of others, we are simultaneously removing obstacles to our own liberation.

If we are ever to discover our true God-given identity, we must respond to this struggle for a just society and true community. We are called to a wholeness as human beings that is much greater than our identity as individuals. This wholeness cannot be fully discovered outside of justice in our society. What we are beginning to learn as non-poor people is that we, no less than those who are impoverished and otherwise marginalized, are dehumanized by the systems of oppression. The image of God in us—the image of our true humanity—is scarred because we have learned to coexist with the violence of injustice. None of us can be whole as long as injustice goes unchallenged. God's love for those who are poor is expressed in liberating and healing acts that show the people that God accompanies them. God's love for the non-poor is no less real. This love invites the non-poor to join God on the margins among the impoverished in order to find our true identity in relationship, in community, in the common struggle to transform the world.

Relinquishment and the Abundant Life

The call to relinquishment is grounded in the promise of abundant life and in the language of salvation. It is the essential gospel dialectic of losing one's life in order to find it. What we are asked to believe is a foolish proposition: the gospel promise that we will receive in return far more than what we give up.

> *Peter began to say to [Jesus], "We have given up everything and followed you." Jesus said, "Amen, I say to you, there is no one who has given up house or brothers or sisters or mother or father or children or lands for my sake and for the sake of the gospel who will not receive a hundred times more now in this present age: houses and brothers and sisters and mothers and children and lands, with persecutions, and eternal life in the age to come." (Mark 10:28–31)*

Jesus responds to Peter's need for some assurance that the decision to follow Jesus will not only entail the negative reality of "giving up." He promises that whatever has been relinquished for the gospel will be given back a hundred times more. He promises a harvest "in this present age," so bountiful as to boggle the mind of the peasant farmer.

Who among us can attempt the "negative" work of relinquishment without some positive vision that makes it worthwhile and even possible? How do we let go of many of the things in which we have come to find security, identity, and status, unless we nurture a hopeful, morally compelling vision of what is possible? Without this ability to imagine our society as a true community, or ourselves as transformed human beings, we will not be able to relax our grip on our socioeconomic status quo.

Wendell Berry has said that we are much more easily motivated by what we desire than by what we deplore. The essence of the prophetic task is to articulate a vision of the common good that has the power to capture the imagination of the people as a goal worthy of struggle and sacrifice. How can we begin to create a vision of our society that makes us willing to move out from behind the walls of our defenses into the unknown but hoped-for future and to stake our lives on such a foolish proposition as the reign of God? For both Jesus and Francis, the vision of the Reign of God was that source of transforming power which animated and informed their sense of mission and community.

Let us now consider the response of the rich man/poor man from Assisi to the gospel call for relinquishment. Francis took the daring leap of faith from a position of privilege into the world of the poor. His renunciation of the world, though radical, was apparently not odious to him. We sense that for Francis the gospel promise was fulfilled, that what one receives in return is far more than what one has given up. Francis renounced the world only to have it given back with joy.

It was not long after his break with family and social life in Assisi that Francis was joined by others who formed with him a community among the poor. The story of Francis teaches us that the invitation and challenge to relinquishment are extended not just to individuals but to communities. We recall that the invitation to the rich man in the Gospel was to join the discipleship community as it traveled along the way. The work of relinquishment is difficult for individuals to realize in isolation. In community we cultivate a common vision that facilitates relinquishment. Community gives us the support necessary to take those steps out of our comfort zones toward the margins of society.

Like that rich man in the Gospel we are generous, we support the "right" causes, and we can list the laws that we have obeyed as "good, moral people." If we adopt this posture, we will never really understand the gospel invitation before us. We can invoke rational arguments for moderation and good sense against the way of Jesus and the way of Francis. This is understandable, for there is something foolish and risky, even senseless, about this path. It is even scandalous! How can a way that seems so negative promise the kind of delight, joy, and abundant life that Jesus promised and Francis found?

Once again we find ourselves invited by Francis to be fools. Is it really possible that what is given up will be returned a hundredfold? Can we believe that as we lose ourselves, we will find ourselves? Francis, who renounces his claim on all things, is free to enjoy all things as gift. Utterly foolish. Impractical. Subversive. Even dangerous.

We can neutralize the challenge and promise of Jesus and of Francis by elevating Jesus and Francis into the realm of sainthood and perfection, a realm seemingly far beyond our reach. Or we can ponder their way of living in the world and attempt to follow them, fools though we would be. It is probably impossible to extract from Francis a precise formula for achieving this kind of freedom. We tell the stories of Francis and of Jesus because we cannot do what we cannot imagine. By telling these stories, may we at least come to imagine that a different way is possible; that we can actually live the gospel; that we can be free of the tyranny of possessions; that we can experience joy in the simple gifts of life and of each day; that we can surrender our lives to a purpose larger than ourselves; that systems exploiting some to benefit others can be challenged and transformed; and that we can dare to work with hope for the transformation of the world toward justice and earth's healing. In telling the story of Francis, we place ourselves in the presence of one who, in losing his life, found it; who in giving up the world received it back transformed; who discovered Christ mysteriously hidden and revealed among those whom society has cast to the margins. We dialogue with one who believed along with Jesus that with God "all things are possible."

OUR STORIES

Reflect on your childhood and adolescence.

• What significance did having things and buying things have in your family?

• How important were material possessions, educational level, professional accomplishments, and social status in your family and community? By what markers of social status or other values did you come to evaluate yourself and other people? Where did you get those values? What else can you remember about attitudes toward possessions and social status?

Reflect on your adult life.

• In what ways have you internalized your culture's voices regarding possessions, economic status, and other indicators of social status? How have those internalized voices shaped your life choices? Have they ever compromised your freedom to choose? Have you ever challenged those internalized attitudes?

• Recall times when you have said to yourself, If only I had a _____, I would be happy. How has that attitude affected your ability to depend on God? or to share who you are? Do you ever respond to anger, depression, sadness, frustration, happiness, or boredom by buying something?

• Can you recall times when you have silently evaluated someone based upon his or her clothing, house, or other material possessions? Can you recall a time when you have been evaluated on that basis?

• In what ways have your attitudes toward material possessions changed throughout your life? Why?

• Do you have a personal relationship with anyone who has chosen to live more simply out of a religious commitment? How do you feel about that person? How has that relationship affected your life?

• Have you a personal relationship with anyone who has a great deal more material wealth than you have? How do you feel about that person? How has that relationship influenced your life?

Signs of Our Times

For much of its history the United States has portrayed itself as a classless society, in which movement from one level of wealth or power to another is quite possible with enough hard work, enough "bootstrap pulling." Until recent decades this illusion was perpetuated by the constant insistence of the dominant group in society that its wealth would "trickle down." At least for those of European descent, the United States seemed to be a land of opportunity.

Beneath the egalitarian surface, however, sharp divisions have plagued this nation since its earliest days. The most pronounced of these is the vast chasm that exists between the ordinary US citizen and a small minority of very wealthy and powerful people. Recent studies confirm what those who are on the economic margins of our society have known all along: wealth in the United States is highly concentrated. The gap is widening, especially since the late 1970s; the rich are getting richer, and the poor are getting poorer. The gap between the richest and the poorest US citizens is now greater than at any time since the Census Bureau began collecting data in 1947. As we write, the wealthiest 1 percent owns nearly 43 percent of financial wealth (defined as net worth excluding the value of one's house), while the bottom 80 percent owns only 7 percent (Domhoff).

African Americans, Native Americans, and other minority groups experience an increasing marginalization that has erased much of the hope engendered by the civil rights movement. Hispanic and black workers earn far less than white workers. The wage gap between white men and Hispanic and black women is vast. While a few US citizens became much richer, many more—disproportionately people of color and women—were thrust more deeply into poverty.

Climate change may become the most widespread manifestation of white privilege and economic privilege the world has ever known. While people of the global North (per capita) have consumed the most fossil fuels and benefitted from fossil-fuel-based industrialization at the root of climate change, the world's colonized and impoverished people are being killed and displaced by it. That reality will only deepen. For example, the Maldives, a nation of islands no more than a mile wide at any point, is threatened with the loss of its entire land mass, forcing the entire nation to relocate. At the same time, even a slight degree of warming decreases the yield of the world's food staples—wheat, corn, barley, rice—in seasonally dry areas. Subsistence farmers and people with little money will go hungry.

In light of these signs of the times, reflect on your economic status and your climate-change status.

• What words would you use to define your economic status?

• Consider the following: If the world were a global village of one hundred people, over seventy of them would be unable to read, and only one would have a college education. Over fifty would be suffering from malnutrition, and over thirty would live in what we call substandard housing. Six of them would be from the United States. Those six would have half of the village's entire income; the other ninety-four would exist on the other half. How would the wealthy six live in peace with their neighbors? Surely they would be driven to arm themselves against the other ninety-four—perhaps even to spend, as we do, more per person on military "defense" than the total personal income of the others.

• Does seeing yourself in these terms as part of the global community alter your initial response? If so, how?

• The typical US citizen produces over 100 times the amount of greenhouse gas emissions in a year than do many of earth's people. In assessing their carbon footprint (the approximate measure of climate-change-causing greenhouse gas emissions caused by a specific person or group in a given period of time) many US citizens find that it would take five to seven—or even more—planets to sustain life if all of earth's people lived as we do. Given our carbon footprint and our society's disproportionate causal role in climate change, what would it mean to call the victims of climate change our neighbor, whom Jesus calls us to love?

• How do you view your current economic status? your level of material possessions? If your basic needs are not being met (you cannot afford for yourself or your family health care, housing, nutritious food, transportation, and so on), how does that affect your self-image? How do you feel about more affluent US Americans?

INVITATION TO RESPOND

In the two exercises that follow, we invite you to enter into a process of self-examination and response. You might do these exercises alone, but we encourage you to engage them in community with others.

Exercise One

Imagine a world in which all people had the necessities for a life with dignity and no one accumulated vast wealth at the expense of others. The path toward this future—the work of justice making—seems overwhelming in its complexity. However, that complexity may seem less daunting if we break it down by recognizing that change happens at four levels:

- personal or household

- corporations and other businesses

- institutions of civil society (churches, universities, school systems, and so on)

- government or public policy

Change at these four levels is interdependent; change at one level enables change at the others.

Imagine how you can be an agent of relinquishment and change toward economic justice in some way at each of these four levels. The following steps will help you in this process:

1. Do an inventory of the resources available to you in at least these dimensions of your life: personal/family life; parish/congregation/faith community; work or professional life; citizenship. Be sure to include human gifts of time and talent; economic, political, and cultural resources; and access to different circles of influence.

2. Using these resources, what primary commitment have you made or could you make toward change at each of the four levels noted above?

3. How does your commitment at one of these four levels open doors to change at any of the other levels?

4. Now, in community with others, make commitments to take steps forward on one or more of the commitments that you identified in Step 2 above. How might you support one another in these commitments? Plan a date in the near future on which you will check in with one another

to celebrate your faithful moves and to note what gets
in your way and how you might support each other in
overcoming those obstacles.

Exercise Two

Do an assessment of your carbon footprint. How many planets
would it take to sustain all people at your level of carbon consumption? (For assessing carbon footprint, see http://www.nature.
org/greenliving/carboncalculator/index.htm.)

Our carbon footprints are so high largely because of our dependence on petroleum. Petroleum is an ingredient of our every
waking moment—from the sheets on our beds, to the floors or
carpets that our feet touch upon arising, to the plastic items in the
kitchen, to the energy that constructed our homes, to the roads
on which we drive, to the electricity that runs our appliances and
gadgets, and more. Yet the economies of the future, if there is to
be a human and humane future, will not be based on petroleum
or other fossil fuels. The petroleum era is a short period in human
history, only a few centuries long.

Imagining a petroleum-free future is the first step to arriving
at it. Talk with your faith community, colleagues, and friends
about the shape of a future not based on carbon emissions. What
will everyday life look like? What source of energy will fuel our
energy needs?

Imagine that you are a part of creating that future. Work
through steps 1–4 above to help you in this process, but where
the steps previously called for you to consider economic justice,
replace that idea with earth-healing through reducing petroleum
dependence.

3

Francis and Community

Living "As If"

In those days he departed to the mountain to pray, and he spent the night in prayer to God. When day came, he called his disciples to himself, and from them he chose Twelve, whom he also named apostles: Simon, whom he named Peter, and his brother Andrew, James, John, Philip, Bartholomew, Matthew, Thomas, James the son of Alphaeus, Simon who was called a Zealot, and Judas the son of James and Judas Iscariot, who became a traitor. (Luke 6:12–16)

The community of believers was of one heart and one mind. . . . They had everything in common. With great power the apostles bore witness to the resurrection of the Lord Jesus, and great favor was accorded them all. There was no needy person among them, for those who owned property or houses would sell them, bring the proceeds of the sale, and put them at the feet of the apostles, and they were distributed to each according to need. (Acts 4:32–35)

FRANCIS'S STORY

*Francis left the town one day to meditate out of doors and
as he was passing by the church of San Damiano which was
threatening to collapse with age, he felt urged to go in and
pray. There as he knelt in prayer before a painted image
of the Crucified, he felt greatly comforted in spirit and he
eyes were full of tears as he gazed at the cross. Then all
of a sudden he heard a voice coming from the cross and
telling him three times, "Francis, go and repair my house.
You see that it is falling down." Francis was alone in the
church and he was terrified at the sound of the voice but the
power of the message penetrated his heart and he went into
ecstasy. Eventually he came back to himself and prepared
to obey the command he had received. He was quite willing
to devote himself entirely to repairing the ruined chapel of
San Damiano." (St. Bonaventure, no. 1)*

*St. Damiano's Church is that blessed and holy place where-
in the glorious Religion and most excellent Order of Poor
Ladies and holy virgins took its happy beginning some six
years after Francis' conversion, by the means of this same
blessed man; whereof the Lady Clare, a native of the city of
Assisi . . . was the foundation. (Celano, First Life, no. 18)*

No dramatic pathways opened for Francis immediately after
his conversion. He simply took what he deemed the next right
step, then the next. He began repairing rundown churches in the
region of Assisi, believing that this was what God wanted of
him. Little did he realize that before long it would be the church
universal that he would repair, in company with hundreds, then
thousands, of men and women who wished to walk Francis's
way. How long this period of solitude and physical activity lasted
is not clear. Soon enough, however, it became apparent to the

young Assisian that his was not to be the life of a hermit, but that followers would flock to his side.

> *Among these, a man of Assisi of pious and simple spirit was the first devoted follower of the man of God. After him brother Bernard, accepting the embassage of peace, ran eagerly after the Saint of God to purchase the Kingdom of Heaven. . . . And straightway another man of Assisi followed him—one right praiseworthy in conversion, who after a little while completed in a yet more holy manner that which he had begun in a holy manner. And after no long time he was followed by brother Giles, a simple, upright and God-fearing man. (Celano, First Life, nos. 24–25)*

The young Francis realized that he was attracting followers and was being called to provide some basic structure for them. In the Prologue we recounted the delightful story of Brother Masseo, who much later in the movement cried out at seeing the throngs who flocked to the brother and sisterhoods: "Why after you, Francis, why after you?" The only answer one can offer is that this astounding growth in the Franciscan movement was the work of God's Holy Spirit.

> *Blessed Francis, seeing that the Lord God was daily increasing the number [of the brethren] for that very purpose, wrote down simply and in few words for himself and for his brethren both present and future a pattern and rule of life, using chiefly the language of the holy Gospel. . . . So he came to Rome with all the said brethren, longing exceedingly that what he had written might be confirmed by the Lord Pope Innocent III. (Celano, First Life, no. 32)*

The first rule of life that Francis proposed to Innocent—and which won the pontiff's approval—was essentially the gospel itself, especially gospel texts that describe how Jesus's followers are to go about in this world. (A *rule of life* in Roman Catholic terminology refers to the guidelines that inspire and guide a particular religious order or congregation.) Francis's rule of life appears to interpret the gospel almost literally. What Francis was doing, however, was appropriating creatively the gospel for his own time. The way of life he set out for his community allowed for differences between his time and that of Jesus. For example, Francis's rule forbade Franciscans to ride horseback—an elitist activity in the thirteenth century. At the same time, his adherence to the gospel remained basic and all-embracing. It was the soil, the air, and the environment for the life of Franciscan communities. Their life was entirely Jesus centered.

As Francis's community life took shape, definite characteristics began to emerge corresponding to the signs of those times. In fact, they would mark the movement forever.

Characteristics of the Franciscan Communities

The most innovative hallmark of Franciscan men's communities may have been their *lay character*. Francis was not an ordained priest; nor was the group that gathered around him predominantly clerical. There were priests among these first followers and, of course, among those who came afterward, but from the start it was a fraternity, a community of brothers.

Clare and the Poor Ladies who joined the movement were a lay sisterhood. In this, Francis followed the actions and words of Jesus at the Last Supper when he washed the feet of his disciples (John 13:14).

The emergence of a brotherhood and sisterhood in which clerics and laity lived together as equals challenged the church to its very foundation. Despite many aberrations in living out this charism through the centuries and attempts to clericalize the

Franciscan order, it has remained in its ideal state a non-clerical order of brothers and sisters.

This leads us to a second very important characteristic of early Franciscanism: its *inclusion of women*. Clare was among Francis's first followers, a great gift to the young order that profited from her gifts and those of the women who followed.

It is worthy of note that, despite the paternalism of that time and place, Francis encouraged Clare to create her own rule and community for the sisters. These Poor Ladies, as they were known, came from all social classes, even the poorest. This was a departure from the norm of that day when candidates for women's religious communities arrived with substantial dowries, thus adding to the wealth of the institute and giving these daughters of the wealthy an even higher station in society.

In tracing the characteristics of Franciscan community life, the influence of Clare can be seen clearly throughout.

Francis's acceptance and embrace of Clare and her sisters in this new way of religious life mirrors Jesus's own example, when, for example, he commissioned Mary Magdalene and the other Mary to announce the good news of his resurrection to the disciples: "Go and tell my brothers to go to Galilee, there they will see me" (Matt 28:10).

Again, Francis's community chose a life dedicated to *action and contemplation* outside of the prevailing monastic tradition of the time. Until Francis, men and women who wished to dedicate their lives to God as vowed people had only one option: to leave the world and enter cloistered monasteries. This unbreakable tradition had held sway for at least seven hundred years before the man from Assisi burst on the scene. Francis broke this mold by remaining in the world, understanding his vocation as a call to the streets, witnessing to the good news of incarnation and salvation, as much as a call to retirement and prayer. One famous story about Francis tells how he went out one day with another brother to preach. The two walked through Assisi for some time, then returned to the friary without having spoken a word. When Francis's companion asked about the saint's intention to preach, he replied that their very presence on the streets was the sermon.

Thus was born a model for religious (vowed) life that remains still: activity flowing from contemplation—contemplation informed by activity. After Francis, the vowed life would never be the same. In this he must have found inspiration in Jesus's prayer to his Abba at the Last Supper: "I am not asking that you take them [Jesus's followers] out of the world, but I ask that you protect them from the evil one" (John 17:15). While it is true that Clare had to retire to the cloister, since the idea of active women religious was incomprehensible at that time in church history, Clare did join Francis at the beginning and is identified with him as co-founder of the Franciscan movement.

Another characteristic of the original Franciscan communities was that they took people interested in this new way of life *exactly where they were*. In Francis's mind, for example, no one had to leave the married state or a particular professional calling in order to follow Christ. Thus, in addition to the brothers who followed Francis (First Order) and the women who joined Clare (Second Order), people with family, social, and professional obligations could join the community as Secular Franciscans (Third Order). Given the usual understanding of religious life in that time, this acceptance of a person's state in life as compatible with full membership in the Franciscan family signified a radical departure from accepted ways—and an entirely new understanding of dedicated life. (*Dedicated life* in the Catholic tradition refers to a commitment to live the gospel as a member of a religious community.)

Jesus's own inclusiveness surely inspired Francis. The Savior had disciples from all walks of life, and he displayed total respect as well as tolerance for the concrete situations in which people found themselves. He received the Pharisee, Nicodemus, for example, when the man was too afraid to approach Jesus in the daylight. He went to the home of the wealthy tax collector Zacchaeus and even pronounced salvation on his household. He ate at table with Simon the Pharisee, challenging him only when Simon and the other men in the room judged a woman as not worthy to be in their presence. For Jesus, discipleship meant not so much a radical change of a person's vocation as a totally new way of living it out.

Characteristically, Francis community operated in a *collegial style*. The lay, non-ordained saint naturally led the group as founder and visionary. But he was also "your little brother" who looked after the brotherhood and sisterhood as a "mother loves and nourishes her carnal child" (St. Francis, "Rule of 1223," VI). While he rigorously upheld his ideals and wishes for the Order, his manner especially toward errant brothers proved eminently gentle.

Such collegiality, however, could not have been free of problems. Even the very early church and the ideals claimed for it in the Acts of the Apostles—quoted at the beginning of this chapter—either existed for the briefest time or not at all. In St. Paul's First Letter to the Christian Community at Corinth, written within twenty-five years of Jesus's death, the Apostle severely criticizes the community members for presuming to celebrate the Eucharist when some are going hungry while others eat too much. With the first Franciscans the saint's leadership was challenged. He once resigned as minister general of the Order. Yet ideally and generally in practice, Francis's leadership in the Order was exercised as a ministry to the collective. In fact, friars in positions of authority, even those who followed Francis in general leadership, held the title of ministers rather than superiors. (A *superior* in Catholic religious parlance does not connote superiority but rather responsibility and authority in the community. Nevertheless, because of its etymology the word has never enjoyed widespread usage in Franciscan circles.) In this we see reflected Jesus's own thinking:

> *"You know how among the Gentiles those who seem to exercise authority lord it over them; their great ones make their importance felt. It cannot be like that with you. Anyone among you who aspires to greatness must serve the rest; whoever wants to rank first among you must serve the needs of all. The Human One has not come to be served but to serve—to give his life in ransom for the many." (Mark 10:42–46)*

Despite the unavoidable daily problems and occasional clashes of personalities inherent in community life, it does seem that the early Franciscans strove to practice love, gentleness, and forgiveness within their ranks. Led by Francis and his understanding of himself as "mother," they bore one another's burdens and spoke the truth to one another. They were from all accounts *communities of great joy*.

Another innovation of Francis's growing communities centered on the custom of *begging for their sustenance* when other forms of support proved insufficient. In the monastic movement theretofore religious had always worked to support themselves, and Francis carried on that tradition. He went so far as to condemn as "Brother Fly" a brother who would not work. But startlingly, the saint moved so deeply into solidarity with the destitute that he and his brothers accompanied the poor even in the humiliating activity of begging when their work failed to produce enough to live on. Leonardo Boff cites this custom of begging as the final step on Francis's journey toward the poor: not only assisting the poor and not only being in solidarity with them, but ultimately becoming poor. The appellation mendicant (beggar) thus came to describe this new kind of religious order.

This fundamental characteristic of the Franciscan community found its inspiration in the text from Luke's Gospel, one which so influenced Francis: "Take nothing for the journey, neither walking staff nor traveling bag; no bread, no money. No one is to have two coats" (Luke 9:3).

Francis also assumed a posture of pacifism: his community was *not to engage in violence* of any kind. This empowered Francis to serve as a reconciling force in situations of conflict. For example, it was Francis who mediated and eventually healed the serious conflict between the bishop and the mayor in Assisi. Francis strove to bring about reconciliation between the Sultan of Egypt and the Crusaders. In his constant meditation on Jesus's sufferings and death, Francis surely took his inspiration of non-violence from Matthew's Gospel, in which at the moment of his arrest Jesus chided Peter, who would defend him with violence: "Put your sword back into its place; for all who take the sword will perish by the sword" (Matt 26:52). This characteristic of Francis's communities is most evident in the rule he set out for lay people who wished to follow him, but because of their life's vocations were prohibited from living in a friary. On these Third Order members Francis laid a strict prohibition against bearing arms.

Francis's *pacifism* should not be confused with *passivity* (we will explain this more fully in Chapter 5). For example, he could become very angry and take dramatic steps when he felt that his God-inspired vision for the Order was threatened or undercut. On one occasion, upon discovering that well-intentioned people of Assisi had constructed a large house of stone and mortar for the friars, Francis climbed to the tiled roof and ordered other brothers to join him in destroying it.

Finally, the emerging Franciscan communities *challenged the Roman Catholic Church* of that time. Initially, church authorities felt uneasy about another group of "zealots" who proposed to "rebuild the church." There were quite enough of these already, and they very often signified a real threat to the institution. Gradually, however, as Francis showed himself and his band to be totally loyal to the church, he received acceptance even at the highest levels of the Roman communion. His earliest rules contained admonitions urging obedience to bishops and to "the Lord Pope." Early on he went to Rome with his first followers and received the formal approval of Pope Innocent III for this new way of religious life. On the other hand, Francis's simple and concrete living of Jesus's gospel, his espousal of Lady Poverty, and his stark, almost literal imitation of Jesus proved to be an enormously challenging and renovating force in the church. In fact, Francis has been called the first Protestant because of his reform from within the body of the church. He saw such reform as always necessary, given the frailty and sinfulness of that human institution. He and his companions walked a most difficult path: remaining in a sin-filled church while offering it a prophetic challenge. He and the first Franciscan communities served as a constant critique of the church, living as they did the gospel without gloss, a witness that called the entire household of faith to the same. To the church's ostentation, inattention to the poor, neglect of pastoral responsibilities, complicity in its own violence and that of the state, and its general state of decline, the emerging Franciscan movement offered both a strong condemnation and a corrective. It was the communal example of Francis and his followers, rather than rhetoric, that offered the critique and provided the challenge.

Jesus had given the example long before. A devout Jew, he insisted that he had come not to repeal the laws of that religion but to fulfill them. Yet his obedience to God's will and his announcement of the reign of God proved an enormous threat to the socioreligious power structure of that day. Jesus became entirely too much for them to bear, and the Jewish authorities finally concluded: "If we let him go on like this, everyone will believe in him, and the Romans will come and destroy both our holy place and our nation. . . . It is better for you to have one man die for the people than to have the whole nation destroyed.

. . . So from that day on they planned to put him to death" (John 11:47–48, 50, 53).

Following Francis, Following Jesus

Church Institutions Today

Much of Francis's genius in developing his gospel-centered communities remains lacking in institutional churches today. Francis's appreciation of the laity and the gifts of women, his integration of contemplation and action, collegiality, simplicity of life, and his rejection of violence, to name just a few, remain ideals our modern church life has yet to attain. At the same time, in every Christian denomination the Spirit is moving—often among grassroots Christian communities, but at times at an institutional level as well.

Our era has been called the age of the laity, and indeed, recent decades have seen an increase in the appreciation of the laity's contributions to the body of Christ and to building God's reign on earth. Yet much remains to be done. Through their baptism lay women and lay men become fully members of the body of Christ, with rights and responsibilities inherent in their lay vocations. But too often ordination to the clerical state is the source of power in the church and lay people tend to function in service to or in function of a priestly caste—a situation that clearly calls for change.

At the same time, in many parts of the church, women's contributions to church life have only begun to receive recognition. One wonders what Clare's place would have been had she lived today. Would her passion, intelligence, and steadfastness to the ideals she shared with Francis have been called forth in our time in ways that were impossible when she lived? While many Christian denominations are inclusive of women, Catholic women are not alone in being denied ecclesiastical equality. The struggle for their rightful role takes place not only on a personal level, but also in relationship to church structures that are often a countersign to the gospel itself. Many Roman Catholics perceive this structural sin in the absolute denial of priestly and episcopal ordination to women.

For Francis and his followers to integrate contemplation with life in the world meant a radical departure from the normal, cloistered religious life of that time. Today, however, the single most recognizable integrating factor in Christian spirituality may be the practice of contemplation in the midst of the world. Almost without exception Christian churches are engaged in significant efforts to alleviate suffering and need; many also are active in the public square, educating and advocating for social justice, peace, and respect for the integrity of creation. In the United States and around the world, trade justice, the rights of migrants, food security, debt cancellation for impoverished countries, human trafficking, and climate change, to name a few areas of concern, are on the churches' agenda. Contemplation is at times integrated into this faith-based action, whether public or private, and vice versa, but there remains a need for growth here among both contemplatives and activists.

Many churches also have far to go with regard to such characteristics of the Franciscan movement as collegiality, simplicity of life, and the rejection of violence. The Roman Catholic Church's authoritarian spirit, which Franciscanism challenged in the thirteenth century, unfortunately remains very much with us today. Other churches, too, regard authority as privilege rather than as service. It is interesting to note the joy engendered in people of faith when such a misreading of gospel authority is corrected by the emergence of a true servant leader. Witness the enormous impact Pope Francis made on the churches from the beginning of his tenure as bishop of Rome.

Similarly, austerity in the use of things—that overriding Franciscan trait—is practiced more by way of exception in the churches, even by Franciscans. At the same time, a growing awareness that excessive consumption is unjust and unchristian in a world where poverty abounds, and unsustainable on a limited planet, is encouraging the churches to reexamine the need for grandiose structures and extravagant lifestyles. Furthermore, financial transparency and public accountability are expected of the churches and every other institution or organization accepting donations from the public.

Finally, despite good faith rhetoric and the efforts of some members working through Pax Christi, many denominational peace fellowships, and other groups—and with the exception of the traditional Christian peace churches such as the Quakers, Mennonites, and Church of the Brethren—many churches have yet to instill in their people the ideal of nonviolence and active pacifism, especially with regard to participation in war. The development and promotion of just-peace theology with the encouragement of the World Council of Churches and the study of faith-based peacebuilding in religiously rooted universities around the world suggest important new institutional movement in this regard.

Significantly, however, evidence points to the decline of mainline denominations, especially in Europe and North America. In the Roman Catholic Church the sexual abuse by clergy and its cover up by authorities in many dioceses and religious orders have risen to the level of scandal in the biblical sense of the word and have understandably driven away uncounted numbers of congregants. No less scandalous are the cases of such clergy violations in other denominations. This cancer will affect the churches for generations to come.

Further, the churches have frequently failed to serve the need that modern people feel for a gospel message that speaks to the times in which we live. Elizabeth Johnson in *Quest for the Living God* describes how the great Jesuit theologian Karl Rahner lamented the irrelevant preaching of his time. By and large, messages from the pulpits of our churches today continue to alienate the hearts of people rather than nourish them.

Finally, modern people often express a desire less for religion (church affiliation and life) than for spirituality. This results in an overall decline in the number of people identified with any given denomination. (Studies of Roman Catholicism in the United States reveal that its aggregate number of adherents would have sharply declined in the past few decades were it not for the enormous increase in Latin American Catholics in our country.)

OUR STORIES

From our earliest days all of us have formed part of communities, though we may not have recognized them or called them that. The immediate and extended family, the neighborhood, the schools we attend, formal and informal groups of which we are a part, our social and working circles—each of these collectives demonstrates that we are social beings, called to be in relationship with others.

In many places today the desire for community has intensified. Twelve-step programs as well as self-help, support, and therapy groups are signs of this phenomenon. For people of faith, the growing awareness that the priorities of our society often stand in opposition to Christian values has produced in them a thirst for faith-based community. Some people have become involved in or actively seek the kind of base Christian community that has burgeoned, for example, in Latin America.

Some people today actually live in faith-based communities. Other people of faith today actively seek a Christian community with which to relate. Many of us have experienced church-based communities—for example, parishes, congregations, Bible study

groups. Consider the following questions in light of the characteristics of the early Franciscan communities: gospel based, lay,
inclusive, democratic, poor, nonviolent, and prophetic.

• What lessons for life have you learned from your participation
in family, neighborhood, and other forms of community?

• Think about one or two experiences of community you have
had. Were they positive? negative? Reflect on these experiences.

• Do you sense within yourself a longing for more intentional
community among people of faith today?

SIGNS OF OUR TIMES

Many people are envisioning a kind of resurrection from the
ashes for institutional church life in our day. Loren Mead has
pointed to the fact that as the churches move from the center
to the margins of society they are reoccupying the vital social
location of the early church and perhaps its prophetic voice.
Phyllis Tickle discerns a pattern in modern church life that has
repeated itself virtually every half century: a kind of garage sale
where the accumulation of theological and political debris is
discarded. Philip Jenkins regularly notes the explosive growth
of the churches in the global South, reminding us that perhaps it
is there that we should look for hope.

In light of Professor Jenkins's observations we must cite the
burst of hope for the institutional churches that another Francis
represents. In an amazingly short time Pope Francis not only
put a new face on the Roman papacy but gave witness to the
moral power that resides in organized religion well lived. Pope
Francis of course is a product of the church in the global South,
a fact that most media commentators overlooked. His life par-
alleled the history of the churches in Latin America with their
breakthrough liberation theology, their call for an institutional

preferential option for the poor, their cultivation of base Christian communities, their understanding of structural/social sin and the need for communities of faith to combat it. Pope Francis immediately began to reflect all of this and more in approaching the global ministry to which he was elected in March 2013. To cite just one or two of this Francis's more important pastoral gestures:

• At the moment of his unexpected election, the pope first and foremost asked the crowds in St. Peter's Square to bless and pray for him—an act acknowledging the people of God and himself as their servant. He chose not to take up residence in the papal apartments but to live in community at Domus Santa Marta. He laid aside many of the traditional trappings identified with the "supreme pontiff," such as a luxurious automobile, ornate liturgical vestments, and the protection of the plexiglass "popemobile." He made perhaps his most famous statement when asked about people with a homosexual orientation: "Who am I to judge?"

• The phenomenon of this pope from the global South seemed to claim the attention of the entire world. It stands as yet another example of the Holy Spirit at work in the churches when something new, different, exciting, and above all, relevant was desperately needed. In reflecting on Pope Francis one is reminded of Martin Luther, Dietrich Bonhoeffer, Dorothy Day, Martin Luther King—and, of course, Francis of Assisi.

And so we come full circle to Francis and Franciscan communities as inspirations for the much-needed rebirth of church institutions. The experience of Francis, though distant in history, provides a ray of hope for such a new springtime.

Community Today

Today, just as in the time of Francis, the Spirit is raising up countercultural Christian communities at a time when God's people most need the support and challenge such gatherings can provide. This community of communities, as it is called, strives to live *as if* the priorities of modern society did not hold sway; *as if* the values of God's reign were already operative in modern society. Such communities witness to the new heavens and the new earth prophesied in the book of Revelation.

The experience of Francis, though distant in history, provides a ray of hope for this new movement. Today, too, there is a need to "rebuild my church," and the rebuilding promises to take place in and through authentic communities, whether inside or beyond institutional churches, which will engage with society as a whole, like the prophets of old, and speak the truth of God's reign to temporal power. God seems to be calling forth groups of communities—a community of communities—to take up today's version of Francis's vocation. The sheer size and complexity of modern life go far beyond any individual's capacity to confront it all. So the community and the community of communities, the churches, become a crucial way of fulfilling the mission of proclaiming and promoting God's reign on earth, as well as denouncing all that stands in the way of that divine *project*. The community is more than the sum of its parts when it understands itself as truly in mission to a seriously wounded world.

In such communities we join with scores of faith-filled women and men to live the great political and theological *as ifs*. Politically, we live *as if* our nation were true to its foundational documents of liberty and justice for all; *as if* people mattered in themselves and not for their economic or social status; *as if* consumerism and the shopping mall did not determine the meaning of our lives; *as if* our way of life were not dependent on fossil fuel; *as if* we were a sister nation among all the other countries of the world; *as if* right made might and not the other way around. Living out these *as ifs* in the midst of community creates a prophetic possibility at a local level, the space for modeling how things could be, ought to be, and one day will be. The characteristics of St. Francis's communities on which we have been reflecting give us a blueprint for such *as if* living.

Theologically, Franciscan communities, like so many others populated by good-willed people of faith, live *as if* God truly exists and calls us to be co-creators of God's reign on earth; *as if* God cared enough about us to send the Only Begotten One to share our journey on earth; *as if* the true Messiah went the way of the cross and came through it as the Risen One; *as if* that resurrection makes all the difference in the world; *as if* we were truly living out this hope.

Some faith communities are practicing the arts of community organizing to build egalitarian communities dedicated to racial justice, economic justice, and ecological sustainability. Some practice the Eucharist and baptism as radical acts of inclusion and grace. Others build alliances with people of other faith traditions who have shared values and commitments to justice, nonviolence, and care for the earth. The movement takes many forms. Some are mainstream congregations or parishes moved by a spirit of faithful renewal. Others are new starts or church plants, exploring what it means to follow Jesus in each new time and place. Green congregations and green seminaries burgeoning across the country are another face of this profound and hopeful renewal.

INVITATION TO RESPOND

All of us inevitably form part of communities—family, social, working, and worshiping communities. They do not always see themselves as true communities, much less as the building blocks for the community of communities, the churches. Keeping in mind, however, the example of Francis and the possibility that a similar grace is being offered to the churches in our time, we are called to break free from our individualism and become more intentional in living these community experiences.

This is especially true of our worshiping community. There we gather regularly to express publicly our deepest convictions about God, ourselves, and society. We profess our faith each time we join others for prayer, reflection, scripture sharing, inspiration, and action. Why can we not pursue this communitarian aspect of liturgy by forming smaller groups for a more intense and mission-oriented life together?

Explore with the parish or congregation to which you belong the possibility of becoming a community of communities. This would mean a different pastoral approach by church leadership. Smaller "house churches" would gather between Sundays for prayer, discussion, Bible study, and mission. On Sunday all these little gatherings might congregate in an act of fellowship and universality. The experience of traditional, primarily Roman Catholic religious orders and congregations stands as a valuable resource in the formation of new, gospel-oriented communities. Like Francis himself, the members of religious congregations are decidedly loyal to the institutional Roman Catholic Church but, like the saint, enjoy and insist upon a certain independence from that institution particularly regarding the manner in which they organize their community life and the ministries in which they engage. This kind of loyal opposition represented by Catholic religious congregations through history seems to be another "well-kept secret" in a denomination popularly known for its monolithic structures. Much can be learned from the long experience of Catholic religious life in the formation of community today. The women and men who live out today the Franciscan charism, for example, are beneficiaries of a centuries-old experience in living community. Their movement within the Roman Catholic Church has survived for over eight hundred years, and today's members carry that institutional memory in their corporate life. They have observed most of what community means, are not surprised at its unpredictability, and thus possess much wisdom for communities forming today. Also, the richness and creativity in one's faith life enabled by such a participative model of church has been demonstrated already in the base Christian communities in Latin America and elsewhere. They also serve as guide and mentor for communities today.

In our working environment, too, the notion of community, while less common and surely more difficult than in a church environment, has rich possibilities. Gatherings of professional or business persons have been tried, often for the sole and somewhat restricted purpose of shared prayer. Less common, but as important, would be Christians coming together to discuss their faith in the context of the workplace. Here there are people of faith facing similar ethical and moral problems. Can we not seek out one another and form groups to discuss and assist one another with the complex choices that the office, factory, boardroom, or hospital presents in terms both of personal conscience and social morality?

Consider the following questions:

• Does the community of communities with which you are familiar—the church—possess some or several characteristics of the Franciscan communities outlined in this chapter?

• Do you find that there is a new call or longing for community among people of faith today?

• Has there been an outward focus or sense of mission in the communities to which you have belonged? Or have they been essentially inwardly focused?

• Are you now involved in a community? If not, is it because of personal temperament? lack of a sense of calling? inability to find a community suited to you? some other reason?

• After reading this chapter, do you feel inspired to form part of an intentional Christian community? Or would you rather not engage in community at this time in your life? How does your response sound to you in the light of this reflection on Franciscan communities?

• Imagine for yourself a community as you would like to see it. What ideals would you wish to see lived out in such a community?

• Have you ever formed part of an intentional Christian community in your workplace? Think of coworkers who might welcome such a venture.

4

Francis and Transforming Friendship

Loving with Open Hands

Six days before Passover Jesus came to Bethany, where Lazarus was, whom Jesus had raised from the dead. They gave a dinner for him there, and Martha served, while Lazarus was one of those reclining at table with him. Mary took a liter of costly perfumed oil made from genuine aromatic nard and anointed the feet of Jesus and dried them with her hair; the house was filled with the fragrance of the oil. (John 12:1–3)

When he was in Bethany reclining at table in the house of Simon the leper, a woman came with an alabaster jar of perfumed oil, costly genuine spikenard. She broke the alabaster jar and poured it on his head. There were some who were indignant. "Why has there been this waste of perfumed oil? It could have been sold for more than three hundred days' wages and the money given to the poor." They were infuriated with her. Jesus said, "Let her alone. Why do you make trouble for her? She has done a good thing for me. The poor you will always have with you, and whenever you wish you can do good to them, but you will not always have me. She has done what she could. She has anticipated anointing my body for burial. Amen, I say to you, wherever the gospel is proclaimed to the whole world, what she has done will be told in memory of her." (Mark 14:3–9)

FRANCIS'S STORY

On one occasion, at Clare's insistence and after much consideration, Francis agreed that they should share a meal. This example of friends drinking deeply of the joy of intimacy stretches our thinking about the impact of such love:

St. Francis had the table laid upon the naked earth as was his custom. And when meal time came, St. Francis and St. Clare sat down together, and one of the Brothers with the companion of St. Clare, and next all the other brothers, and they humbly took their places at the table. And with the first dish St. Francis began to talk of God so lovingly, with such depth, so wonderfully, that the divine fullness of love descended upon him, and all were enraptured in God. And while they were thus transported with eyes and hands lifted toward heaven, the people of Assisi and Bettona and in the neighboring towns saw that Santa Maria degli Angeli and the whole convent and woods, which then were at the side of the convent, seemed to be in a great blaze. (Jörgensen, 120)

Thomas of Celano tells another story about Francis's availability for and generosity in friendship. It is included here because it illustrates the importance and gratuitousness of true friendship. Brother Riccerio imagines himself unworthy of Francis's love but discovers not only that he is already loved deeply by the Poverello, but also that such love is neither reward nor recompense, but rather pure gift.

A brother named Ricerio, noble by birth but nobler by conduct, a lover of God and a despiser of himself, was led, by the eager wish of a dutiful spirit, perfectly to attain and possess the favor of holy father Francis, but he greatly feared that in consequence of some hidden judgment St. Francis shrank from him and therefore made him a stranger to the favor of his love. That brother considered (being a God-fearing man) that if St. Francis loved any one with the deepest charity, such a one would also be worthy to deserve God's favor, but that, on the other hand, any one to whom St. Francis did not show himself well disposed and benign would fall under the wrath of the judge on high. These thoughts the said brother kept turning over in his mind, of these things did he frequently hold silent converse with himself, disclosing the secret of his cogitation to none.

But one day, when the blessed father was praying in his cell, and Ricerio was come to that place distressed by his wonted cogitation, the Saint of God both knowing of his arrival, and understanding his thoughts at once sent for him and said, "Let no temptation mislead you my son; let no cogitation afflict you, for you are most dear to me, and know that among those specially dear to me you are worthy of my affection and intimacy. Come in to me confidently whenever you will, and let my friendship give you confidence to speak." Ricerio wondered with the utmost amazement, and thenceforward having become more reverent, as he increased in the holy father's favor, so he began to have a larger trust in God's mercy. (Celano, First Life, nos. 49-50)

Perhaps we can only discover the significance of intimate relationships in the lives of Jesus and Francis by intuition and implication from a few concrete details, from legends that so often reveal the soul of reality, and from our growing comprehension of the thoroughly grounded, deeply rooted humanity of each.

Jesus and Intimacy

Among the most important biblical stories offering direct suggestions about the role of friendship in Jesus's life are the accounts of Jesus's visits to Bethany, a village on the other side of the Mount of Olives. Recall for a moment Jesus's visit there in the home of Mary and Martha (Luke 10:38–42), Jesus's "safe house" where he went to enjoy deep friendships; to explore with his friends the profound implications of his message; to rest and be renewed—encouraged—to continue his own prophetic mission; and to invite and to challenge them to walk with him on the journey. Mary's "better part," that of total absorption in the balm of deep friendship, may amuse (even irk) those of us who find ourselves so often setting the stage of life, preparing the meals, cleaning, and creating the possibility for life to move on gracefully. But Jesus's invitation to Martha to share in the delicious fruits of friendship gives clear indication of the pleasure and fulfillment he experienced therein.

In John's Gospel (11:1–44), Jesus again visits Bethany, for "Jesus loved Martha and her sister and Lazarus" (John 11:5). There he was confronted with the death of Lazarus:

> *When Jesus saw her [Mary] weeping and the Jews who had come with her weeping, he became perturbed and deeply troubled, and said, "Where have you laid him?" They said to him, "Sir, come and see." And Jesus wept. So the Jews said, "See how he loved him." (John 11:33–36)*

Beyond companionship of the sort that Jesus must have shared with the fishermen and others who formed the immediate community of disciples around him, the Bethany stories highlight

Jesus's celebration of life-giving intimacy with both men and women.

Brazilian feminist theologian Maria Clara Bingemer, reflecting on John's story of Jesus's anointing at Bethany (12:1–3), describes the effusive and permeating aroma of perfumed oils as Mary pours them over Jesus's feet. Her bold intrusion, her interruption of the way things were already arranged in terms of table fellowship, gives powerful and concrete witness to the penetrating presence of women in Jesus's life. The anointing of Jesus's feet and Mary's drying of his feet with her hair would have been extremely unusual actions in the Jewish community of Jesus's day. A woman never appeared in public with her hair unbound, and the familiar action of welcome for dinner guests was to anoint their heads, not their feet. John wanted to underscore the extraordinary display of love and gratitude contained in Mary's lavish gesture.

In Mark's (14:3–9) version of this incident (which is probably more historically accurate), an unnamed woman pours expensive perfumes over Jesus's head. Like the gesture of love and gratitude described in John's Gospel, this woman's action of anointing was in itself prophetic proclamation. This anointing with oil, the identification of the one who was to initiate the inbreaking of the reign of God, was a dangerous action in the tense historical context of Jesus's entrance into Jerusalem. By this action, which was defended publicly by Jesus, the woman moved from a position at the margins of Jewish society onto center stage.

In *Binding the Strong Man* Ched Myers underscores this point and notes that this dear friend of Jesus, the woman, courageously confronts the approaching death of the one she loved. The woman anoints Jesus's body in anticipation of his death, in "ideological solidarity" with the way of the cross.

One can imagine the gift that such deeply intimate encounters were in the life of the One who was soon to face the cross. At Bethany Jesus surely received encouragement and deepened his own resolve to move forward toward the final confrontation with religious and civil authority and finally to his death on the cross.

Over the objections of some who witnessed the loving action of anointing with expensive oils, Jesus defended the woman, saying that the "poor you will always have with you," a passage often misunderstood as an excuse for avoiding actions of solidarity and the struggle for justice. However, the mission of Jesus and his followers had by that time been clearly articulated; the divine option for the poor had been proclaimed. Perhaps Jesus was suggesting that the reign of God must include, but is more than, the struggle for social justice—it is seen as well in moments of merciful intimacy. In fact, without the gift of intimacy, the work for social transformation can become an arid and dehumanizing exercise. The reign of God is built within oneself, between oneself and others, and in social structures as well. In this conversation Jesus gave particular focus to the intimate dimensions of the New Creation task.

Jesus's celebration of women was of a piece with his celebration of the marginal ones of his time, but it went beyond that. He welcomed them into the life-giving circle around him, aware that their presence was essential at the heart of the discipleship community—that without their inclusion, the shalom was not possible. He learned from women as well as from men the possibility of life-giving relationships; he relied upon them, too, for healing and courage; he explored with them the implications of his mission; he received from them the gift of accompaniment even to the foot of the cross; and he appeared first to them when he had overcome the forces of evil and risen from the dead. The mutuality of his relationships with women was symbolically but clearly documented by the evangelists. Women demanded of Jesus his healing power (the woman with an issue of blood), delighted in his attention (Mary, while her sister Martha was busy about so many things), claimed his respect (the woman at the well), even challenged the ethnocentric worldview of his day (the pagan woman who insisted on a cure for her daughter)—and he reciprocated in every instance.

In Jesus one sees the results of this capacity for intimacy with both women and men. His appreciation of intimate relationships allowed him to show great tenderness to a widow whose only son had died (Luke 7:11–17). How he acted (tenderly) was as important as that he acted (politically). It made him sensitive to a woman with an embarrassing hemorrhage (Matt 9:20–22 and parallels) and to one taken in the act of adultery (John 8:3–11).

At the same time, Jesus's capacity for enabling friendship was glue for the ones who followed him through tremendous stress for three years. His openness to love was part of his charisma, and the strength of the love he received in return helped him confront the weakness of the religious leadership of the day.

Francis and Intimacy

So it was with Francis. Surely his mother, Pia, then Clare and Jacoba (an older woman and close friend who visited Francis when he was dying, bringing sweet cakes and great love), brothers Leo, Bernard, and Juniper, and many others nurtured in him the sensitivity for which he is so noted. So many times we read of this most disciplined and austere person breaking his fast and setting the table himself when a brother seemed at the point of utter exhaustion from want of food. We see Francis anticipating his brothers' needs, as exemplified in the story of his concern for Brother Riccerio. Despite the challenges of a demanding way of life, the Franciscan brotherhood strove to be a community of gentleness and love. In the writings of Francis,

> *the word brother is used more than any other (242 times), almost always accompanied by an adjective of affection: "my most beloved brothers," "my blessed brothers," "my brothers." His care and tenderness were so intense that he*

*was loved like a "most beloved mother." And essentially
that is how he acted. (Boff 1984/2006, 33)*

Other friendships fostered the rigorous side of his personality:
Clare's witness to austerity must have deepened Francis's own
embrace of a sparse religious life, while his friendship with the
friar Illuminato helped sustain him on the dangerous journey
toward the Sultan of Egypt, Malik al-Kamil, the one feared by
all Christians and target of the Fifth Crusade. In fact, the biographies and legends of Francis suggest the possibility of deeply
loving friendships in Francis's life beyond his own fraternity,
especially with Clare.

Twelve centuries after the time of Jesus the place of women
in society had not improved, and one is easily overwhelmed by
the heavily negative attitudes of Francis's day toward women
and their bodies. On the one hand, Clare's journey seemed to
follow some of the most apparently self-denigrating and negative
traditions of Catholic religious life. For example, the symbolic
act of cutting off her hair (and Francis's participation in that) as
she joined the "brotherhood" is breathtaking when considered
in the light of feminist thought today. Moreover, it would seem
to contradict the essence of the Franciscan insight: that all of
creation (women's bodies included) is pure gift and possesses the
innate capacity to glorify God. On the other hand, as we delve
more deeply into Clare's appropriation of the lifestyle suggested
by Francis and her articulation of that journey for and with the
women of her own community, it becomes clear that Clare was
a woman who pushed back the boundaries of women's religious
life in her time and challenged the Franciscan brotherhood to be
faithful to its own vision of poverty as well. She was clearly an
extraordinary woman, and her gift to Francis was that of calling
him to risk the humanizing journey of intimacy.

Clare's strength of character helped greatly to shape the community that had gathered around the Poverello. She expected

from Francis respect and mutuality, and he offered her both. She gave him great love, and he loved her deeply in return. The legend of the flowers that bloomed in the snow—when Francis suggested that he and Clare should see each other again only when winter was over and the roses returned—symbolizes the depth and strength of their love for each other:

"Francis and Clare were never separated" means that both were so united in the same evangelical endeavor, so strongly tied to a third reality above and beyond them, the poor Christ, his Gospel, and the service of the poor, that essentially nothing would distance the one from the heart of the other. Both had their heart anchored in God. Because of this, space and time did not count for them. . . . The love that they had for each other, always excelled by the love of both for the poor and for Christ, made them spiritual twins. When Francis had doubts about his own vocation, he charged Clare and her sisters to pray to God for light. And when she suffered pressures because of the "privilege of radical poverty" . . . Francis also worried with his whole heart. (Boff 1984/2006, 31–32)

The story of the meal shared by Francis and Clare is also fascinating, and highly symbolic. According to the biographer Jörgensen, the shared meal was Clare's idea; she insisted that they should have the opportunity to be immersed in the pleasure of each other's company and friendship. This insistence was not a weakness but a bold response to her own instinctive understanding of the importance of intimate moments between good friends, of the fact that the very presence of the beloved is a tremendous gift reflective of the presence of God, and of the need for such moments for nourishment of the spirit.

The meal was shared with others as well. This is a requirement for life-giving relationships: to love with open hands in such a manner as to embrace the world, especially the world of marginalized people so essential to the Franciscan way. And the bread they broke bore the fruit of communion with the Holy One—fulfillment of the deep, respectful, faithful touching of souls that can happen in human relationships. "Love of the one for the other bursts toward the heavens, toward God, without ceasing to be, in everything, a profoundly human love" (Boff 1984/2006, 32).

Intimacy as a Source of Renewal and Joy

Francis and Clare also sought each other's companionship when the burdens of life became unbearable. When he was desperately ill, Francis returned to San Damiano to be near Clare and her community. It was in those bleak moments when he was in terrible pain, yet bathed in the light of their friendship, that he was inspired to write the Canticle of Creation, a remarkable testament to a profound renewal of his spirit.

Francis's fulfilling relationship with Clare and his deep friendships with the brothers may well have inspired the beautiful masculine-feminine interplay in the Canticle of Creation. Francis composed the canticle while he was desperately ill and convalescing in a small hut next to San Damiano, close to Clare and her community. The wholeness of creation is reflected in the integration of masculine and feminine in the Canticle. Although the feminine and masculine characteristics described by Francis reflect the biases of his times (the feminine as "useful, lowly, precious and pure," for instance), the Canticle sings of a fullness that reflects and honors the plan of God.

Jesus's retreats to Bethany and his plea to his friends the night of his arrest that they watch one hour with him suggests that he also had a deep need for human companionship. His hour had come, and he would drink of the chalice poured out for him. But his soul cried out for friendship and understanding in that very situation. Twice he rouses the sleeping eleven, repeating the request for accompaniment. Had they responded, Jesus's burden, loneliness, and fears would have lessened. He would have been able to face his approaching torments knowing that his friends were with him. Friendship—intimacy—is most needed in our difficult hours and, when shared, lifts our spirits and enables us to move on.

FOLLOWING FRANCIS, FOLLOWING JESUS

Anyone who has loved deeply knows how miraculously the heaviness of life can be lifted in an encounter with the beloved. The gift of joy is poured forth in great abundance in the context of love. Like Francis and Clare, friends can encourage each other to live the gospel with fervor and integrity, to stay on the discipleship journey even when the challenges of doing so are great.

The Gift of Close Friendship

Close friendship can be a great treasure. But in the past, new members of Catholic religious communities, who were preparing to make a vow of celibacy, were often warned against "particular" friendships. While examples of inappropriate intimacy abound in our world today—some of which could be perceived as a threat to other life commitments—it is important to claim the great gift of deep friendship in our lives and to lift up the examples of Jesus and of Francis. In both we find the capacity for special relationships revealed.

Jesus visited Bethany where he found hospitality, understanding, and love with Martha, Mary, and their brother, Lazarus. This was especially true near the end as he made his way inexorably toward the Holy City and his final hours. He also had special friends among the apostles: "the disciple whom Jesus loved"

(John 13:23); "he took Andrew, Peter, James, and John to a high mountain and was transfigured before their eyes" (Mark 9:2); "Simon, son of John, do you love me more than these?" (John 21:15).

Francis, too, demonstrated this same capacity for particular friendships and for the loving attitude toward all of humanity that flows from them. We can love all people only in the measure that we love particular persons well, and this Francis did. He obviously loved Clare intensely, and she returned his love; theirs is one of the many great love stories among Christian saints. That Francis also loved his brothers in varying degrees only underscores the special nature of each relationship. Particularity is a hallmark of love that is neither dangerous nor inappropriate but enhances the lovers' capacity to embrace the rest of the world.

Intimacy as a Source of Courage

What was the significance of intimacy for the lives and mission of Jesus and Francis? What might that say in our own times?

Jesus's anointing at Bethany took place shortly before his confrontation with religious and civil authorities brought him face to face with death. His renewal at Bethany encouraged him to take the next step toward Jerusalem. The prophetic oils of the woman's love strengthened him and affirmed his commitment to the path that God had set for him.

As men and women began to gather around Francis in love and friendship, he must have found in them a new source of inspiration for his dream. Now he would not walk alone; he would be gifted with these friends who shared the vision of radical gospel living. The young Francis was encouraged by Bernard and the others to ask the Roman ecclesial authorities to approve their way of life.

Francis's friendship with Clare deepened and nourished the vision of the beloved community, with all of its prophetic dimensions, of which they were both a part. They turned to each other when the road became unbearably difficult and found in their love the possibility of taking another step.

True friendship and deep love embolden the beloved to renewed fidelity to the gospel expressed in the concrete actions and choices of life. It thrusts us toward the world, a world so often in excruciating pain. At the same time, it nourishes our capacity to move through the suffering and to believe in the possibility of transformation. Intimacy is the place where grief is made bearable and where we find the strength even to face death.

Intimacy as a Source of Revolutionary Accompaniment

Jesus's friends not only sent him forth with renewed courage to Jerusalem, but they also, especially the women, went with him to Calvary and beyond. So many of those men and women who followed Jesus paid dearly for their friendship with him and for the discipleship journey upon which they embarked at his invitation. First John, then Stephen, Peter, Agnes, Felicity, Perpetua, and so many others returned Jesus's great love by loving him very well—even unto death.

Such a friend for Francis was Illuminato, the friar who, according to Bonaventure, went with Francis to meet Sultan Malik al-Kamil of Egypt. Francis surely chose him carefully because of a deep bond of trust between them. They would spend some two years together in the riskiest circumstances, facing the possibility of death.

Clare's fidelity to the gospel must have been a great challenge to Francis; together they walked toward the margins to accompany those with no choice but to dwell there. She lived the vows in the most radical sense, totally dependent on the charity of others, precluded even from begging because of the women's cloistered life. She embraced fully with Francis the poverty of those who suffered in the society of their day. Their love for each other required of them the risks of a revolutionary journey.

Friendship in the service of the New Creation is mutually enabling of radical choices to participate in the work of social transformation. It nurtures our capacity to love deeply and is a necessary inspiration without which the path of discipleship is almost impossible. It is food, blood, and life source for those who would participate in the transformation of the social structures of our world. Life-giving intimacy thrusts us toward action for social change—toward families, communities, societies, and a world constructed to enable the inbreaking of the reign of God. The experience of love fills us with a desire for the good.

Friendship as a Place of Accountability

The deep love between Francis and Clare evoked mutual accountability to vocation and commitment. Clare left her family to follow the Poverello, and her radical interpretation of religious life must have challenged the brotherhood, even Francis himself, in return.

Our deepest friendships offer us the possibility of confronting in ourselves the inclinations to stray from the journey toward New Creation by catching a glimpse of the powers and principalities operative in our own lives. Truly loving and respectful confrontation toward genuine accountability in Christian discipleship is most possible in the safe place of intimate relationships. And intimate friendships cannot remain life-giving for long if mutual attentiveness to the demands of fidelity to the gospel is not woven into the fabric of loving interaction.

Intimate Friendship: A Place to Meet God

A wonderful passage in the book of Genesis contains the words of Jacob upon meeting his brother, Esau: "To come into your presence is for me like coming into the presence of God"

(Gen 33:10). The fire of unbounded love offers an incomparable taste of the New Creation. A song from *Les Misérables* repeats this lovely notion: "Take my love for love is everlasting. . . . And remember the truth that once was spoken, to love another person is to see the face of God."

The more deeply we experience intimacy with another person, the more likely we are to be open to the love of God. Jesus and Mary Magdalene, Francis and Clare did this. We simply have to put aside all of the fears and second thoughts that the offer of intimacy brings. Despite the acknowledged risks that relationships carry with them, they are from God. They have been entered into by the Clares and Francises of history, and they are the one surest safeguard from the sterile individualism that so afflicts modern society.

There are important links between intimacy and spirituality, between life in God and life in another. Life in God, for example, requires an other-centeredness not unlike selfless friendship. Life in God requires that we move our centers of gravity outside of ourselves to dance the dance of life with all peoples and all of creation. Intimate friendship calls us to dance that dance with the other as well. Life in God requires that we risk all in the cosmic effort to live justly. Intimacy requires risk as well—in the miraculous discovery of mutually respectful, life-giving, and just relationships.

Our Stories

Choose one important and intimate relationship with which you have been blessed in your life and answer the following questions as you reflect upon it:

• How have I been challenged to personal growth by this relationship?

• Has this relationship pushed me out toward a suffering world or pulled me into private space?

• How did we challenge each other to be more faithful to the gospel, especially to the social dimension of the gospel?

• In what ways did I meet God through this relationship?

SIGNS OF OUR TIMES

There is perhaps no area of life in which human beings have so consistently failed to apprehend and follow the example of Jesus as the area of human relationships. Herein lies, perhaps, the fundamental problem at the heart of the social crisis. Let us look carefully at the particular characteristics of US society that make intimacy difficult or impossible. Among these we might emphasize inbred patterns of domination, various forms of separation, an intense spirit of competition, the fragmentation of families and friendships by work and other activities, and the derivation of identity from occupation or possessions. There are many other forces that tear apart relationships; we all know them well. Technology is a mixed blessing. On the one hand, social media, cell phones, and hyper-connectivity can interfere with immediate "in person" relationships; on the other hand, they can strengthen real but long-distance relationships, which don't have the support of frequent person-to-person contact.

The industrialized West has deep roots in patterns of domination from which it is almost impossible to break. We are only now beginning to apprehend the horrifying consequences of our traditional behavior—from our images of God, of our relationship with God, and even of God's innate characteristics, to our patriarchal patterns of thought and communication—from our cultural roots to our political, economic, and social patterns of organization. Without honoring the dignity of others, we simply cannot foster intimacy and mutual respect in a relationship. Whenever one person dominates and the other must act in subordination, mutuality and life-giving intimacy rooted in justice are precluded.

Similarly, racism, sexism, homophobia, and religious-ethnic exclusionary behavior militate against intimacy. The barriers that separate us from other classes or groups of people ultimately separate us as well from those whom we desire to love and cherish. It is only when we open our hearts to all people, when we pull down the walls that divide us from our brothers and sisters who are different from ourselves, that we are open to intimate relationships with another as truly equal.

Until quite recently in our society, males in particular were schooled from birth until death in a competitive spirit. Lately that emphasis has been somewhat moderated; yet, in general, as a people, we believe that competition brings out the best in us, whether in athletics, studies, or work. From the time our children can walk they are introduced to competitive games. Sports that are good for our bodies are used to nurture our winning spirit as well. Grades in schools are used to encourage students not only to do their best, but also to come out at the head of the class. In business we strive to climb the ladder of success, to get ahead of our competitors. And our nation, by whatever means necessary, has to believe itself to be Number One.

Surely there is a place for the spirit of competition. But in a society where the competitive spirit has gotten out of control, it may well be impossible to cherish the "other" because we are trying so hard to get ahead of him or her. Relationships that truly honor the other's gifts are becoming extremely rare.

The frenetic pace of life in this society has many causes. Many of us work to survive, sometimes at two or three meaningless and low-paying jobs. Others work long hours to get ahead. Still others are so dedicated to the cause for which they struggle that they never come up for air. In addition, other activities consume inordinate amounts of our time and energy. Many are worthwhile; others are not. Regardless, it is a common complaint in the United States that there is no time left for leisure—even for the leisure of the relationships that would nourish our very existence. Some would say we are in a time famine.

Who we are is defined much too often by what we do or have. This phenomenon is perfectly understandable. It is what we teach one another all the time. We ask, "What do you do?" not "What do you care about?" And Madison Avenue is incredibly convincing with its lessons about having in order to be.

> *The culture of lost interiority is paradoxically a culture of lost intimacy. Alone with our passive aloneness, but not in true solitude, we find that our ability to relate to other persons has atrophied. We know not how to give ourselves to the other since it is an empty fortress we call the self. And we know not how to receive the other's love, since one cannot love what one does not know. (Kavanaugh, 10)*

Look with care at the advertising on the Internet, in magazines, on television, or in the newspaper. Keep a list of what the advertisers say you will "become" if you buy their products or if you accomplish a particular task or feat. As *Time* magazine asserts, "We are what we eat, what we build, what we buy"—or, as a bumper sticker tells us, "I shop; therefore, I am."

INVITATION TO RESPOND

Take some time to think about who you really are and about the most wonderful characteristics of someone very close to you.

• Is there something that keeps you from intimacy, even with this person you love?

• How can you learn to celebrate the other, to listen to the other in your life with care and respect?

• How can you learn to challenge each other gently toward radical discipleship?

• What choices could you make together that would move you in this direction?

Francis and Nonviolence

"A Force More Powerful"

*"Blessed are the peacemakers,
for they will be called children of God."
(Matt 5:9)*

*"But I tell you, love your enemies and
pray for those who persecute you." (Matt
5:44)*

*Then Jesus said to him,
"Put your sword back into its place;
for all who take the sword
will perish by the sword." (Matt 26:52)*

FRANCIS'S STORY

Every fiber of Francis's being seems to have been transformed as he attempted to appropriate Jesus's way life into his own journey. His embrace of the leper and radical conversion to the side of impoverished and excluded neighbors were matched in fervor by his commitment to peace. The "Admonitions," a collection of Francis's best advice to his followers on a variety of topics, and the "Rule of 1221" both reflect the integral nature of peacemaking to the Franciscan life, as do multiple stories in the early biographies.

Preaching Peace

Francis, therefore, Christ's valiant knight, went round the cities and fortresses proclaiming the Kingdom of God, preaching peace, teaching salvation and repentance for the remission of sins, not with plausible words of human wisdom, but with the learning and power of the Spirit. The Apostolic authority which had been granted him enabled him to act in all things with greater confidence, without using flattery or seducing blandishments. . . .

Men ran, women too ran, clerks hastened, and Religious made speed to see and hear the Saint of God who seemed to all to be a man of another world. People of every age and either sex hastened to behold the wonders which the Lord was newly working in the world by His servant. Surely at that time, whether by Holy Francis' presence or by the fame [of him], it seemed that, as it were, a new light had been sent from heaven on earth, scattering the universal blackness of darkness which has so seized on well-nigh the whole of that region, that scarce any one knew whither he must go. For such depth of forgetfulness of God and such slumber of neglect of His commandments had oppressed almost all that they could scarce endure to be roused, even slightly, from their old and inveterate sins.

He darted his beams like a star shining in the gloom of night, and as it were the morning spread over the darkness; and thus it came to pass that in all short time the face of the whole province was changed, and she appeared of more cheerful countenance, the former foulness having every-where been laid aside. (Celano, First Life, nos. 36, 37)

Blessed are the peacemakers, for they shall be called the children of God (Matt 5:9). They are truly peacemakers who are able to preserve their peace of mind and heart for love of our Lord Jesus Christ, despite all that they suffer in the world. (St. Francis, "Admonitions," XV)

The Bishop and the Mayor

Toward the end of his life Francis responded to a public, violent conflict in Assisi that began between Mayor Oportulo and Bishop Guido. The bishop had excommunicated the mayor for entering into agreements forbidden by the pope that had re-ignited war with Perugia, but this was not a "misunderstanding or argument between the bishop and the mayor." According to Pace e Bene's account in *Franciscan Nonviolence*, the conflict "reflected serious structural challenges involving the nobility, the new merchant class, the commune, and the Church." In his efforts to resolve the conflict, "Francis seemed to have an intuitive understanding of this. While fully aware of the demonic nature of the institutions of his times that caused so much bloodshed, poverty and suffering, he also addressed the deeper spiritual disease, the thirst for violence, the lack of a sense of reverence for God's creatures, and the failure to appreciate the gift of Creation" (Butigan, Litell, and Vitale, 42).

At that same time when [Francis] lay sick, the bishop of the city of Assisi at the time excommunicated the podestá [the mayor]. In return, the man who was then podestá was enraged, and had this proclamation announced, loud and clear, throughout the city of Assisi: no one was to sell or buy anything from the bishop, or to draw up any legal document with him. And so they thoroughly hated each other.

Although very ill, blessed Francis was moved to pity for them, especially since there was no one, religious or secular, who was intervening for peace and harmony between them. He said to his companions: "It is a great shame for you, servants of God, that the bishop and the podestá hate one another in this way, and that there is no one intervening for peace and harmony between them." And so, for that reason, he composed one verse for the Praises:

> *Praised be you, my Lord, through those who*
> *give pardon for your love,*
> *and bear infirmity and tribulation.*
> *Blessed are those who endure in peace*
> *for by you, Most High, they shall be crowned.*

Afterwards he called one of his companions and told him: "Go to the podestá and on my behalf, tell him to go to the bishop's residence together with the city's magistrates and bring with him as many others as he can."

And when the brother had gone, he said to two of his other companions: "Go and sing the Canticle of Brother Sun before the bishop, the podestá, and the others who are with them. I trust in the Lord that he will humble their hearts and they will make peace with each other and return to their earlier friendship and love."

When they had all gathered in the piazza inside the cloister of the bishop's residence, the two brothers rose and one of them said: "In his illness, blessed Francis wrote the Praises of the Lord for His creatures, for His praise and the edification of his neighbor. He asks you, then, to listen to them with great devotion." And so, they began to sing and recite to them. And immediately the podestá stood up and folding his arms and hands with great devotion, he listened intently, even with tears, as if to the gospel of the Lord. For he had a great faith and devotion toward blessed Francis.

When the Praises of the Lord were ended, the podestá said to everyone: "I tell you the truth, not only do I forgive

*the lord bishop, whom I must have as my lord, but I would
even forgive one who killed my brother or my son." And
so he cast himself at the lord bishop's feet, telling him:
"Look, I am ready to make amends to you for everything,
as it pleases you, for the love of our Lord Jesus Christ and
of his servant Francis."*

*Taking him by the hands, the bishop stood up and said
to him: "Because of my office humility is expected of me,
but because I am naturally prone to anger, you must forgive
me." And so, with a great kindness and love they embraced
and kissed each other. . . .*

*All the others who were present and heard it took it for a
great miracle, crediting it to the merits of blessed Francis.
(Armstrong, Hellman, and Short, 187–88)*

Jesus Christ: Peacemaker

Woven into the fabric of Jesus's story from beginning to end
is an identification of his mission with peace on earth—deep
peace, peace rooted in justice, shalom, and a call to the task of
peacemaking for those who would be disciples.

Jesus's way of life was a model of nonviolence, a deep challenge to the "norm" of the Roman Empire in the first century. His
call was marked by certain very specific characteristics that defined
a culture of peace and love. In fact, the life of Jesus, Word of God,
was given completely to conveying a universal message to his followers and the world: "Peace be with you. . . . Love your enemies
and pray for those who persecute you" (Matt 5:44). "Do to others
what you would have them do to you" (Matt 7:12; Luke 6:30).

Peace be with you. Feed the hungry. Clothe the naked. Visit
the sick and the imprisoned. Give drink to the thirsty. Welcome
the stranger. Love your enemies. Do good to those who hate
you. Turn the other cheek. Sell everything you own and give the
money to the poor.

Jesus modeled a radically new way of life. He did not respond passively in the face of violence; rather, by word and deed he resisted the violence of unjust social structures. He defied laws and rituals that marginalized the poor and ethnic outsiders, proclaimed release to the captives and liberation to the oppressed, extended the messianic message of liberation to the outcasts, and favored those who were poor. As he struggled to overcome the structural violence of poverty and exclusion, his resistance was always nonviolent. He refused violence even as a final resort to save his life, not to advocate passivity in the face of horrific violence, but to take on the violence deliberately and to demonstrate the powerful force of nonviolent love. The spectacular growth of the Christian community in the centuries following Jesus's death and resurrection was surely impelled by the power of his witness to life, even in death.

Love, justice, nonviolence, inclusion, compassion, community, generosity, integrity, peace. Jesus repeatedly modeled the way of peace that he prescribed for his followers:

Bless those who persecute you; bless and do not curse them. Rejoice with those who rejoice, weep with those who weep. Live in harmony with one another; do not be haughty; but associate with the lowly; do not claim to be wiser than you are. Do not repay anyone evil for evil, but take thought for what is noble in the sight of all. If it is possible, so far as it depends on you, live peaceably with all. Beloved, never avenge yourselves, but leave room for the wrath of God; for it is written "Vengeance is mine, I will repay says the Lord." No, if your enemies are hungry, feed them; if they are thirsty, give them something to drink; for by doing this you will heap burning coals on their heads. Do not be overcome by evil, but overcome evil with good. (Rom 12:14–21)

In the years just after Jesus's death, the first Christians— who were mainly Jews themselves—had to deal with the steadily building resistance of their Jewish countrymen against the Roman occupation. Scholars today believe Mark's Gospel was written just before the Jewish revolt in 66 CE to give these first Christians a clear view of Jesus's life and teaching and to help them stand strong against the pressures to join in the revolt. Jesus's clear rejection of violence—from the first time he was tempted in the desert to his refusal to allow the people to fashion him into a revolutionary messiah to the way he dealt with the corruption of his society's leadership to the way he responded to their violence towards him—helped inspire the first Christians to take their stand. They refused to participate in the violent revolt. . . . Jesus's nonviolent way of dealing with hate and violence was normative for them and helped them through their political travail.

In the next era, from the end of the first century to the end of the third century, Jesus's example and teaching helped guide Christians as they dealt with the next most difficult political challenge facing them—violent Roman persecution. Their heroic way of life, a life of love for their enemies and a willingness to suffer for their faith, deeply impressed the peoples of the ancient world. Their example gradually inspired mass conversions to the Christian faith. (Rynne, 2)

The early church advocated a ministry of reconciliation and called upon its people not to return evil for evil. Forgiveness and doing good to all people were to be the norm for God's people. Nowhere in the life of the early Christian community or in the writings of the early church was violence advocated. In fact, as Stanley Hauerwas writes: "From the witness of the early church, Christians did not even find it necessary to declare they were nonviolent—exactly because the way of nonviolence could not be distinguished from what it meant for them to be Christian. . . . Nonviolence was constitutive of the Christian conviction that Jesus is Lord" (Hauerwas, xvii).

For nearly three hundred years the vast majority of followers of Jesus Christ adhered to that norm by refusing to shed another person's blood under any circumstances.

> *And we who were filled with war, and mutual slaughter, and every wickedness, have each through the whole earth changed our warlike weapons—our swords into plough-shares, and our spears into implements of tillage—and we cultivate piety, righteousness, philanthropy, faith and hope. . . . Now it is evident that no one can terrify or subdue us who have believed in Jesus all over the world. For it is plain that, though beheaded, and crucified, and thrown to wild beasts, and chains, and fire, and all other kinds of torture, we do not give up our confession; but the more such things happen, the more do others and in larger numbers become faithful, and worshipers of God through the name of Jesus. (Long, 16)*

That began to change in the Constantinian era (fourth century), and by Francis's time, violent conflict between city-states involving many Christians was a regular occurrence in Italy, and the killing of the Saracens was considered a religious act by the Christian church.

In the Footsteps of Jesus

Remember Francis, the dashing young soldier who fought in the war between Perugia and Assisi and spent long months as a prisoner of war, returning home, sick and disillusioned. Paul Moses in *The Saint and the Sultan* points to the seeds of his call to peacemaking that were evident even while Francis was still captive, as he befriended a prisoner who was both nasty and isolated, bringing other prisoners "to peace with him" (Celano, *Second Life*, no. 4), and showed signs of being affected by a deep aversion to combat (Moses, 33).

In his conversion from a popular, profligate troubadour to an imitator of Christ, Francis rejected all the values of society that led to repeated wars between Italy's city-states and was reborn as a peacemaker (Moses, 34). His commitment to peace and nonviolence thereafter infused his own life and the values of the Franciscan community.

His unusual greeting, "May the Lord give you peace," was a challenge to the lords of war (Moses, 35–36), a call to overcome the violence that was dominant in his times, along with the political and economic structures that fostered that violence (Butigan, Litell, and Vitale, 21).

In adopting for his "personal signature" the Tau cross, Francis clearly rejected the meaning it was given by Pope Innocent as a symbol for his Crusade. He accepted the church's more benign understandings of the Tau as a sign of a "Passover" from sinfulness to holiness and as a sacramental Passover in the reestablishment of Eucharistic centrality in Christian worship. However, he never associated the Tau cross with the crusading movement. According to Franciscan Michael Cusato, "This is compelling evidence—evidence of a conscious and deliberate choice of Francis not to associate the cross of Christ with the crusades, contrary to . . . over a hundred years of the Church doing just that" (Cusato, 90).

As we reflect upon Francis's role as a peacemaker and his deep commitment to nonviolence, we recognize the personal, interpersonal, and political ramifications of his nonviolent lifestyle:

• Francis's poverty moved him to the side of people living on the margins; poverty distanced him and his community from possessions, the protection of which so often provides an excuse for violent conflict.

• His belief in the importance of right relationships among the brothers and sisters who followed him made nonviolence the operative principle in the Franciscan community.

• His repeated efforts to mediate conflict within the larger community of Assisi and neighboring villages demonstrated that his was a commitment to *active* nonviolence.

• His resistance to the Crusades and his journey to visit the Sultan gave witness to his belief in the possibility of nonviolence and respect as basic to the relationships among different cultures and religions.

• His understanding of the brotherhood and sisterhood between humans and the rest of creation reinforced his commitment to nonviolence in those relationships.

• His intense desire to share in the sufferings of Christ led him to the heart of Jesus's witness to the power of active nonviolence that takes on violence, even death, rather than inflicting violence on or killing another person.

On the cross, Jesus overcame sin and evil. His was an active nonviolence that resisted deep injustice and social evil—as he had been doing throughout his public ministry—and that finally led him to his execution on the cross. Jesus's nonviolence in the face of torture did not fit into the belligerent ways of kingdom building many expected but was a sacrifice powerful enough to challenge injustice and evil throughout all of history.

Jesus had modeled another way. Clearly, he did not respond passively in the face of violence; rather, by word and deed he resisted the violence of unjust social structures. He defied laws and rituals that marginalized poor people and ethnic outsiders, proclaimed release to the captives and liberation to the oppressed, extended the messianic message of justice to the outcasts, and favored the poor. Yet his resistance was always nonviolent; he loved even those who would kill him.

> *The means of the old order cannot bring about the ends of the new. Anything less than a politics of militant, nonviolent resistance is counterrevolutionary, a recycling of the old world. Mark's Jesus calls for a more radical (driving-to-the-roots) social transformation, a unity between means and ends. . . . The cross is not only a reminder of the political "cost of discipleship," but can also be seen as a symbol of what Gandhi calls satyagraha. (Myers 1988, 438)*

Francis, too, modeled another way. Where others created enemies, he created brothers and sisters. He embraced peace, apparently rejecting war out of hand. He could do this because he had faced the negative elements within himself. Francis's power as a mediator, reconciler, and bringer of peace was grounded in part in his integration of the negative and the positive aspects of his being. Leonardo Boff, in his discussion of Francis as a model of integration, provides valuable insight:

> *Within every heart abide angels and demons; a volcanic passion shows itself in every human action; life and death instincts abound within every person; desires to reach out, desires of communion with others and of self-giving live alongside the urges of selfishness, of rejection, of meanness. This is especially true of the lives of the saints. If they are saints, it is because they sense all of this not as destructive; but rather, overcoming them by facing them, checking and channeling them toward the good. . . . This agonizing situation can be observed especially in the person of Saint*

Francis. . . . Francis was a saint who integrated the totality of his energies in an archetypal way. The negative especially was included. . . . I believe that Francis—with his perfect joy, with his path of joyful humility, lived within the dark of the senses and spirit—may evoke in us unsuspected powers of harmony and conquest within our own heart. . . . Francis, with this explicit ownership of the diabolic, liberates himself for a total experience of his own reality and so allows for an integration without rejection. (Boff 1984/2006, 116–19)

For Francis, fully and humbly facing the demons within himself was a doorway into a deeper encounter with an infinitely loving God. It brought him face to face with God's mercy, boundless love, and grace, which are ever more abundant than sin.

FOLLOWING FRANCIS, FOLLOWING JESUS

Enormously difficult is the challenge presented to contemporary Christians by the examples of Jesus and Francis. Are we also to reject violence at all costs? Are we to refuse use of a deadly weapon against an invader in our home even if it means loss of our own life or the life of a loved one? Are we to refuse participation in weapons production even if it means losing our savings or our livelihood? Is there such a thing as a just war? Must all followers of Jesus and Francis embrace nonviolence? Even to ask these questions, to face the challenge they present, is extremely difficult because it means swimming against a tremendously powerful current; it means defying the world as we know it.

We, like Francis, live in a society in which violence, both subtle and blatant, is the norm, the way of life, and in some cases even lauded. From our earliest years we are immersed in the affirmation and glorification of violence. Note what our children are exposed to daily, especially in video games. Whether they are destroying the "bad guys," shooting soldiers, or cheering fighter jets soaring across the screen, young minds are being trained to kill in the most proficient manner possible.

Even more pervasive is the warning to be afraid, a message intensified by acts of terrorism or insanity repeated around the world, including in elementary schools, colleges, movie theaters, and many other locations in the United States. The flood of handguns and other small arms in the United States and in many other countries also projects a strong message that violence is the only route to personal security.

The challenge of Jesus and of Francis to live nonviolently is as counter to our culture as it was to theirs. What does it mean to follow in their footsteps?

Are we, following Jesus, called to oppose violent social structures—the violence of a federal budget that stockpiles weapons of mass destruction instead of providing health care, education, and homes; the violence of regressive tax structures or an unjust global economy that allow the rich to grow richer while hunger and homelessness continue to plague too many families, even in our nation's capital? Choosing against violence means that we can no longer ignore or accept the violence of poverty, racism, sexism, militarism, unbridled capitalism, and other forms of systemic oppression—a frightening choice indeed for the non-poor. It leads to the relinquishment of some advantages. It leads to lifestyle choices that others may find strange or threatening. It means devoting time, intelligence, and energy in efforts to confront and change structural violence.

As we experience the difficulty and the fear that accompany this challenge, we are reminded that it is probably not possible to retain a comfortable place in this world and at the same time to follow Christ. Kierkegaard calls the desire to maintain respectability and worldly honor while calling oneself a Christian "wanting to have a mouthful of flour and to blow at the same time."

Christ does not promise peace as the world knows it. What better model can there be for opposing society's demands than Francis?

OUR STORIES

Take some time, preferably with two or three other people, to answer the following questions, which are based on a Pax Christi International process for reflection on the experience of active nonviolence in different contexts:

• Which situation of violent conflict, violence, or war has deeply touched you and/or challenged you? Describe this situation, your own role in relation to it, your feelings, and your responses.

• What was your attitude toward the use of violence in this situation? What was the meaning of nonviolence?

• Describe fully all the steps in a campaign of active nonviolence that was applied in efforts to change an unjust situation or law. Were you a participant or an observer? In either case, what were the consequences of the action?

SIGNS OF OUR TIMES

The nature of violence has shifted in significant ways over time, massively so since the time of Francis. The last century was perhaps the bloodiest in history, with millions of people killed in wars, massacres, revolutions, street violence, assassinations, and terrorist attacks. Violent conflict is no longer the reserve of governments, with non-state actors and irregular armies perpetrating horrific violence at local, national, and international levels. Tools for inflicting violence are readily available for deliberate or accidental use. From handguns to weapons of mass destruction, the human race is well equipped to kill, and our sophisticated capacity for instant communications makes appalling violence highly visible on a global stage.

But destructive violence is hardly limited to murder, terrorism, or war. It also is structural and institutional, including

• *economic violence,* the collective consequences of the economic policies and decisions made in recent years across the globe by choice or under duress that have borne the bitter fruit of poverty, extreme wealth, unemployment and underemployment, hunger, lack of access to potable water and basic sanitation, homelessness, lack of affordable health care and education, overt violence and war;

• *cultural violence,* the potential loss of identity and vision, traditional languages, values and practices as wealthy and powerful societies, in the relentless pursuit of new markets, overwhelm those with less capacity to project themselves beyond a local or regional context;

• *racial violence,* the persistent legacy of white privilege regularly invisible to or ignored by white-skinned people but devastating to people of color;

• *ecological violence,* unsustainable patterns of production, over-consumption, and waste generation at the heart of the current global ecological crises, with earth's resources used, controlled, hoarded, and/or polluted by a few, while millions of the world's people suffer the impact of these losses;

• *spiritual and psychological violence,* the myriad of ways that destructive violence is seeping into the soul of humanity.

Moreover, war often stems from structural and institutional violence: the pursuit of natural resources, including oil, land, water, and all the minerals that drive the current model of "development"; economic injustice; concentrated power; geopolitical or territorial advantage; environmental destruction and climate change; religious, cultural, and ideological intolerance; and on and on.

The impact of war and egregious violence on the well-being of already marginalized people is devastating. Countries affected by repeated cycles of violence—whether the violence is criminal, political, economic, cultural, racial, or ecological—have been largely unable to meet the most basic needs of their poorest people: eradicating hunger, providing good universal education, reducing child mortality, improving maternal health and gender equality, combating communicable diseases, ensuring ecological sustainability.

At the same time, the production, marketing, sales, and trafficking of weapons worldwide is a trillion-dollar business upon which many local communities and even countries depend, or believe they depend, heavily. As a human family we have invested unimaginable talent and treasure in preparations for war.

Is Peace Even Possible?

No doubt, peace is an urgent need. Peace is also, as we know well, much more than the absence of war. So the work for peace is multifaceted, and peacemakers around the world have embraced the challenge. Together they are addressing the root causes of war and the preparations for war; educating for peace; building skills for nonviolent conflict transformation; developing capacity for unarmed protection and peacekeeping; building cultures of peace; investing in diplomacy and negotiation; developing early warning systems to forecast violent conflict; strengthening the rule of law locally and globally; supporting multinational cooperation; and engaging women as peacemakers.

Canadian diplomat Douglas Roche, who served as Canada's Ambassador for Disarmament at the United Nations, writes:

The list of war-torn places that have given way to processes of peace and reconciliation is long: Angola, Ivory Coast,

Mozambique, Guatemala, El Salvador, East Timor, Sierra Leone. All these places have stories to tell of building the conditions for peace. New mechanisms to improve peacekeeping, peace-building, and international justice, many under United Nations auspices, are laboriously being built. This creativity goes largely unreported, and people are unaware of the great strides being made in changing the old culture of war into a culture of peace. Despite the headlines, a new dynamic for peace exists in the world. (Roche, 13)

In the last century the world has witnessed the power of active nonviolence for promoting a more just and peaceful world. Mahatma Gandhi, Martin Luther King Jr., and Lech Walesa are widely known for their vision, leadership, and courage in this regard, but dozens of important examples of nonviolent conflict in recent years exist. Among the most notable are India's struggle for liberation from Britain (1919–45), Danish resistance to the Nazi occupation (1944), the US civil rights movement (1950s–60s), Zambia's liberation from Britain (1961–63), the People Power Revolution in the Philippines (1983–86), the Chilean Campaign against Augusto Pinochet (1983–89), the pro-democracy movement in Hungary (1989), the Singing Revolution in Estonia (1989), the Velvet Revolution in Czechoslovakia (1989), Solidarity in Poland (1981–89), Timorese Resistance in East Timor (1988–99), and many more.

In *Why Civil Resistance Works*, authors Erica Chenoweth and Maria Stephan argue that "historically, nonviolent resistance campaigns have been more effective in achieving their goals than violent resistance campaigns" (Chenoweth and Stephan, 220). Honest political leaders are listening.

Pax Christi, Nonviolent Peaceforce, CureViolence, and many others are working to break cycles of violence and promote cultures of peace.

Faith-Based Peacemaking: Beyond "Just War"

The pursuit of peace is an act of hope. It requires careful theological reflection on the values of our faith traditions in specific situations of violent conflict and war. It requires presence, accompaniment, and the nurturing of relationships across boundaries between countries and cultures, and even neighborhoods. It requires the creation and use of a moral framework and ethical tools that apply the principles of nonviolence in a way that is appropriate to these times and to particular situations. It requires vigorous spiritual exercises, creative liturgical expression, and careful social analysis.

As the very nature of war and destructive violence has changed and the futility and negative consequences of war have become more evident, the role, importance, and potential of nonviolent conflict and peacemaking have come more clearly into focus. Theologians, ethicists, pastors, educators, parents, and many community leaders are calling for a global ethic that would promote the values of nonviolence cultivated in every major religious tradition.

The World Council of Churches (WCC), the Catholic Church, and many other faith communities are deeply engaged in efforts to articulate a moral framework for addressing violence and working for peace. The WCC writes:

> To condemn war is not enough; we must do everything in our power to promote justice and peaceful cooperation among peoples and nations. The Way of Just Peace is fundamentally different from the concept of just war and much more than criteria for protecting people from the unjust use of force; in addition to silencing weapons it embraces social justice, the rule of law, respect for human rights and shared human security. (World Council of Churches 2012, 180)

Religious peacemakers bring particular gifts to the work for peace. Many of them reflect the values Francis brought to his own context of conflict—whether in Assisi and other Italian city-states that were immersed in the violence of perpetual war, or, as we shall see in the following chapter, in the context of the Crusades. Examples abound.

The church of Sudan, for example, accompanied grassroots people through decades of war and violent conflict from 1955 to 1972 and from 1983 to 2005. Church leaders like Catholic Bishop Paride Taban knew the local communities well and understood the roots of what seemed to be unending conflict. Having moved from village to village throughout the war, he gained the utmost trust and confidence of the Sudanese people from north to south and east to west. In 2004, in South Sudan near the Ethiopian border, Bishop Taban organized the Kuron Peace Village. He was determined that peaceful coexistence was possible and began to make it a reality in the peace village, where people from many different ethnic groups and religious traditions have learned to live together in harmony.

In the oil-rich city of Kirkuk, during the US war in Iraq that began in 2003, religious leaders from different traditions, including Christians and Muslim—both Shiite and Sunni—worked consistently together in response to the violence to meet the needs of the community. Whenever an attack occurred, the religious leaders would speak out together in opposition to the violence and in support of those who were harmed. Elsewhere in Iraq, coeducational, interreligious schools brought together Muslims, Christians, Yezidis, and Turkmens to provide a base of human values and an introduction to human rights.

From San Pedro Sula to Los Angeles to Baltimore and San Salvador, people of faith are working with gang members and youth at risk to build nonviolent skills for dealing with conflict and frustration.

And faith-based advocates by the thousands engage decision makers at a national and international level—at the United Nations and the European Union, in Washington, DC, Addis Ababa, and Seoul and everywhere in between—to promote the peace that Francis and Jesus sought.

These peacemakers often bring to the task of building peace a long-term commitment to accompany those whose lives are affected by destructive violence; a recognition that each person, even the so-called enemy, is a child of God; and belief that reconciliation and restorative justice are essential steps on the journey to lasting peace, and that the fullness of peace is the reign of God at work.

INVITATION TO RESPOND

Peace Is Structural and Systemic

Do one of the following exercises with other people:

1. Watch one or more of the films available at www. aforcemorepowerful.org. Identify the values, motivations, characteristics, and surprises in the story or stories in the video. What challenged you? What does this have to do with your own context?

2. Watch one or more of the films on women, war, and peace at www.peaceisloud.org. What is the significance of UN Security Council Resolution 1325 that is a commitment to involve women at every level in efforts to achieve peace and security? How has your country responded to this challenge?

Peace Is Personal and Interpersonal

Francis invites those of us who would be peacemakers to explore our personal inner landscapes through prayer, meditation, honest self-examination, and inner healing. Trusting that God's love for us truly is unconditional—and cannot be lessened by any inner demon—opens the door for this process. Until we begin to uncover and forgive the demons within—those parts of self that are broken, hidden, degraded, or impotent—those demons will express themselves in destructive ways, inhibiting our ability to make peace.

- Read the following *Decalogue for a Spirituality of Franciscan Nonviolence* written by Rosemary Lynch, OSF, and Alain Richard, OFM, slowly (in Butigan, Litell, and Vitale, 47). Reflect on your own journey in this light:

- Learn to recognize and respect "the sacred" ("that of God" as the Quakers say) in every person, including in ourselves, and in every piece of Creation. The acts of the nonviolent person help to free this Divine in the opponent from obscurity or captivity.

- Accept oneself deeply, "who I am" with all my gifts and richness, with all my limitations, errors, failings, and weaknesses, and to realize that I am accepted by God. To live in the truth of ourselves, without excessive pride, with fewer delusions and false expectations.

- Recognize that what I resent, and perhaps even detest, in another, comes from my difficulty in admitting that this same reality lives also in me. To recognize and renounce my own violence, which becomes evident when I begin to monitor my words, gestures, reactions.

- Renounce dualism, the "We/They" mentality (Manicheism). This divides us into "good people/bad people" and allows us to demonize the adversary. It is the root of authoritarian and exclusivist behavior. It generates racism and makes possible conflicts and wars.

- Face fear and deal with it, not mainly with courage but with love.

- Understand and accept that the New Creation, the building up of the Beloved Community, is always carried forward with others. It is never a "solo act." This requires patience and the ability to pardon.

- See ourselves as a part of the whole creation to which we foster a relationship of love, not of mastery, remembering that the destruction of our planet is a profoundly spiritual problem, not simply a scientific or technological one. We are one.

- Be ready to suffer, perhaps even with joy, if we believe this will help liberate the Divine in others. This includes the acceptance of our place and moment in history with its trauma, with its ambiguities.

- Be capable of celebration, of joy, when the presence of God has been accepted, and when it has not been to help discover and recognize this fact.

- Slow down, to be patient, planting the seeds of love and forgiveness in our own hearts and in the hearts of those around us. Slowly we will grow in love, compassion, and the capacity to forgive.

6

St. Francis and the Sultan

Dialogue Across Boundaries

On that day, when evening had come, he said to them, "Let us go across to the other side." And leaving the crowd behind, they took him with them in the boat, just as he was. Other boats were with him. A great windstorm arose, and the waves beat into the boat, so that the boat was already being swamped. But he was in the stern, asleep on the cushion; and they woke him up and said to him, "Teacher, do you not care that we are perishing?" He woke up and rebuked the wind, and said to the sea, "Peace! Be still!" Then the wind ceased and there was a dead calm. He said to them, "Why are you afraid? Have you still no faith?" And they were filled with great awe and said to one another, "Who then is this, that even the wind and the sea obey him?" (Mark 4:35–41)

So, when you are offering your gift at the altar, if you remember that your brother or sister has something against you, leave your gift there before the altar and go; first be reconciled to your brother or sister, and then come and offer your gift. (Matt 5:24)

To cross over the Sea of Galilee signifies much more than crossing a body of water. These journeys at times meant that Jesus and the disciples were crossing a border that separated Jewish and Gentile territory. Jesus calls his followers in the boat to overcome their fears and to find courage and peace in the One who can calm wind and wave. This Francis did quite literally when he crossed the Mediterranean Sea bound for Egypt. Francis exemplifies the possibility and importance of dialogue across religious, cultural, and geographic boundaries. In this the saint lives out the gospel text from Mark recounting one of several sea crossings that appear in each of the Synoptic Gospels as well as in the Gospel according to John.

This gospel story is complemented by the other in which Jesus indicates clearly how his disciples are to act toward anyone they have harmed: "Go, first be reconciled to your brother or sister." We shall see how clearly Francis lived out this directive in his contact and growing relationship with the Islamic leader Malik al-Kamil.

FRANCIS'S STORY

Ernoul, a contemporary of St. Francis and an eyewitness to the Fifth Crusade, wrote the following account:

Now I am going to tell you about two clerics who were among the host at Damietta. They went before the Cardinal [Pelagius Galvani, papal legate of Pope Honorius to the Fifth Crusade], saying that they wished to go preach to the Sultan, but that they did not want to do this without his leave. The Cardinal told them that as far as he was concerned, they would go there neither with his blessing nor under his orders, for he would never want to give them permission to go to a place where they would only be killed.

For he knew well that if they went there they would never come back. But they responded that, if they were to go there, he would have no blame, because he had not commanded them, but had only allowed them to go.

And thus they begged the Cardinal insistently. When he saw that they were firm in their resolve, he told them: "Sirs, I do not know what is in your hearts or in your thoughts, whether these be good or evil, but if you do go see that your heart and your thoughts are always turned to the Lord God." They responded that they only wanted to go [to the Sultan] to accomplish a great good which they longed to carry to its conclusion. Then the Cardinal said it was indeed good for them to go if they wished, but they were not to let anyone think that he had sent them.

And so the two clerics left the Christian camp and headed towards that of the Saracens. When the Saracen sentinels saw them coming they thought that they were messengers or perhaps had come to renounce their faith. When they met them, they seized them and led them to the Sultan. (Marini, 4–5)

The Sultan looked over the odd duo in his tent. Francis and his traveling companion, Friar Illuminato, barefoot monks dressed in coarse patched brown tunics. His soldiers had found the two wandering around the outskirts of the Muslim camp and seized them roughly. Francis and Illuminato had cried out "Sultan, Sultan!" That these unarmed Christians had survived their initial encounter with the Sultan's troops was wonder enough. What could they want?

The Sultan thought that perhaps the Franks, as Muslims called all Crusaders, had sent them to his tent with a response to his latest peace proposal. The Sultan, made weary by war, desperately wanted a deal that would end

*the Christians' siege of Damietta, a city at the mouth of the
Nile where his people were dying of disease and starvation.*

*"May the Lord give you peace." Francis surprised the
Sultan with his words. It was the friar's standard greeting—
most unusual for Christians in his time, especially during
war. It perplexed the Sultan. Uncertain about his visitors'
intention, the Sultan asked if they had come as representa-
tives of the Pope's army.*

*"We are ambassadors of the Lord Jesus Christ," Francis
responded. The Sultan, a subtle, philosophical man who
was schooled in the ways of Christians, could not have
missed the distinction Francis drew in asserting that he was
God's ambassador, not the Pope's. This daring little man
and his companion intrigued him—they even resembled the
severely dressed Sufi holy men the Sultan revered for their
mystical insights into Islam. (Moses, 1–2)*

Historical Background

Before reflecting on the story of Francis's lengthy encounter
with Sultan Malik al-Kamil of Egypt, and its direct relevance for
our times, a word about its historical context.

The visit took place in 1219 and 1220 during the Fifth Crusade, called by Pope Innocent III, which began in 1217 and was
carried out by his successor, Honorius III, after Innocent's death
in 1216. Crusades had been cast in religious terms from their
inception in 1095: holy wars designed to recapture the Christian
sacred places from their Muslim occupiers. No less a figure than
the great Benedictine reformer St. Bernard of Clairvaux wrote
the following in the early twelfth century to Hugh de Payens, a
founder of the Knights Templar:

*It seems that a new knighthood has recently appeared on
the earth, and precisely in that part of it [the Holy Land]*

which the Orient from on high visited in the flesh. . . . Go forth confidently then, you knights, and repel the foes of the cross of Christ with a stalwart heart. . . . I do not mean to say that the pagans are to be slaughtered when there is any other way to prevent them from harassing and persecuting the faithful, but only that it now seems better to destroy them than that the rod of sinners be lifted over the lot of the just, and the righteous perhaps put forth their hands into iniquity. (Bernard of Clairvaux)

These words from such an authority give one an idea of how acceptable these "righteous" wars against Muslims to free the Holy Land had become in the Christian ethos of that time. The fact that in the four years of preparation for the Fifth Crusade (1213–17) Francis, the "*vir Catolicus totus apostolicus*" (Catholic man, entirely apostolic), never once preached or wrote in favor of Pope Innocent's war initiative, despite papal decrees and encouragement for it, speaks volumes about the saint's attitude toward war and presages his action to forestall or at least mitigate the impending violence.

Francis, of course, had tasted the bitterness of war. As a young man he had set forth as a soldier of Assisi to do battle against its neighbor, Perugia. Not only did he fail utterly as a warrior, but he became a prisoner of war for a year, after which he returned to Assisi, broken in body and spirit, for a long period of recuperation. From then on Francis of Assisi was unalterably opposed to warfare; nonviolence was an integral part of his great conversion.

Francis's Mission

The traditional understanding of St. Francis's trip to Egypt and the months he spent in conversations with Sultan al-Kamil has held that it was a stark encounter between good and evil—between Francis, the saint, and al-Kamil, the sinner (or at least a seriously misguided human being). One of St. Francis's earliest biographers, St. Bonaventure, writes:

> *In the thirteenth year of his religious life, [Francis] made his way to Syria where he courageously surmounted all dangers to reach the presence of the Sultan of Egypt. . . . The Sultan had decreed that anyone who brought him the head of a Christian should be rewarded with a Byzantine gold piece. (St. Bonaventure, 702–3)*

However, recent scholarship has revealed that the meeting of these two men was much more nuanced, even complicated. First, there is the question of Francis's motivation. Was he seeking martyrdom in setting out for Egypt and the Muslim world? Scholars find evidence on both sides for this possibility. Another early biographer of St. Francis, Thomas of Celano, wrote that Francis had earlier sought martyrdom when he attempted a journey to Morocco in order to preach to a sultan there. However, later evidence shows that after that aborted trip to the Muslim world for reasons of health, Francis returned to Assisi with exciting plans for the overall future of his Order—hardly the attitude of someone seeking martyrdom. Still, St. Bonaventure seems to indicate that Francis did indeed wish to die for Christ: the thought of death attracted him. On the other hand, a highly respected Franciscan writer, Hugh of Digne, who set out to retrieve Francis's original vision for the Order in the decades after the saint's death, wrote that the friars should be willing to sacrifice all for Christ but to be prudent as well, avoiding violent situations rather than seeking death (Moses, 124). It does seem that the preponderance of scholarship today favors this more benign understanding of Francis's motivation vis-à-vis martyrdom. Nevertheless, the question to some extent still remains open.

Islam

Then there was the entire question of Islam as a religion. Francis could not have been ignorant of the popular (Christian) view of Islam in his time. St. Bernard of Clairvaux continues in the same letter quoted above:

> *Certainly it is proper . . . that those who trouble us should be cut off, and that all the workers of iniquity should be dispersed from the city of the Lord. They busy themselves to carry away the incalculable riches placed in Jerusalem by the Christian peoples, to profane the holy things and to possess the sanctuary of God as their heritage. (Bernard of Clairvaux)*

Pope Innocent called for the Fifth Crusade insisting that the Muslims had befouled the holy places in Jerusalem and the Crusade was a means of imposing God's vengeance on them. However, as we shall see, Francis became increasingly impressed and even influenced by the Islamic religion. While in the Sultan's camp Francis greatly admired the *adhan*, the call to prayer *(salat)* five times each day. The word *inshallah* (God willing) used by Muslims surely influenced Francis, whose own spirituality echoed so completely this sentiment. Clearly, Francis anticipated in a seminal way what eight centuries later the Second Vatican Council would affirm of Islam:

> *The Church regards with esteem also the Moslems. They adore the one God, living and subsisting in Himself; merciful and all-powerful, the Creator of heaven and earth, who has spoken to men; they take pains to submit wholeheartedly to even His inscrutable decrees, just as Abraham, with whom the faith of Islam takes pleasure in linking itself,*

submitted to God. (Declaration on the Relationship of the Church to Non-Christian Religions, no. 3)

Malik al-Kamil

Finally, another and much more complicating factor in the traditional understanding of Francis's journey to Egypt and his lengthy stay in the camp of the Sultan is the Sultan's persona. While al-Kamil's words quoted above about rewarding anyone who would bring him the head of a Christian point to a ruthless man, the reality is not as clear.

Born just one year and a half before Francis, in 1181, Malik al-Kamil was a man of his time, place, and above all, religion. His uncle, known as Saladin, had led a Muslim army to the conquest of Jerusalem; his father, Saladin's brother, was a key strategist in the same Muslim victory, which gave them the city of Jerusalem in the year 1187. At age twenty al-Kamil was appointed viceroy of Egypt by his father and from all accounts made his own fairly prudent governance decisions, even undoing some of his father's. He sought to achieve peace with Christians from the West by means of trade. And throughout the siege of Damietta—the background of Francis's visit to him—the Sultan appeared ready to negotiate a disposition of Jerusalem rather than wage war against the Crusaders.

It does not seem totally out of character, then, that al-Kamil would welcome these two ragged Christian visitors from the West, Francis and Illuminato, when they greeted him with "May the Lord give you peace." From all accounts the Sultan had an inquiring mind. The sight of two barefoot holy men fascinated him and reminded him of both Muslim and Christian holy people. In addition, Francis's greeting of peace echoed the Qur'an: "Say not to those who greet you with peace 'you are not a believer'" (Moses, 130). In addition, the Sultan could well have seen in these visitors a possible bridge to peace with the Christians.

Whatever the Sultan's motives, it is significant that he allowed Francis and Illuminato to remain in his camp for all of a year, while his struggle to save Damietta from the Christian army raged on.

What is more to our purpose here is the effect that Francis's contact with Islam, personified by Malik al-Kamil, had on him. Unfortunately, the hagiography—benign, idealized interpretation—given this subject in the years following Francis's sojourn in Egypt, especially after his death, could not hint at anything positive. It was, after all, an era of Crusades, which would continue throughout much of the thirteenth century. Just as in our time, warring sides could not afford to ascribe humane qualities to the enemy for fear that such an attitude would soften the "necessary" antagonism toward the adversary.

In his homily on the feast of St. Francis in 1262, thirty-six years after Francis's death, a former chancellor of the University of Paris, Cardinal Eudes of Chateauroux, said: "He [Francis] longed so much to die for Christ that he went among infidels to preach the Christian faith and even to the cruel Sultan, in the hope of having to suffer for Christ. But when the Sultan realized this, he refused to make him a martyr in order to deprive him of so great a glory" (Moses, 207). The true facts of Francis's relationship with Malik al-Kamil, however, are distinctly different. The Sultan offered Francis and Illuminato several lavish gifts— "great quantities of gold, silver and silk garments," whether as a bribe or as a genuine expression of respect for these friars' obvious good intentions (Moses, 145). Francis, of course, refused all of these, but the one gift he did take with him on his departure from Egypt was an ivory horn, the instrument used to call the Muslims to prayer five times each day.

Now, at the distance of more than eight hundred years, we have finally come to a much more positive and healthy perspective on St. Francis and Malik al-Kamil. When he heard in 1224, for example, that plans for yet another Crusade were under way,

Francis went into a period of mourning at La Verna. This was a favorite mountain retreat in Tuscany to which Francis often retired for periods of intense prayer and fasting and where, during that summer of 1224, he received the marks of the crucified One, the stigmata.

Thomas of Celano later enfleshed this intense experience when he described how Francis saw a seraph, a vision of what appeared to him as a man with three pairs of wings, fixed to a cross. After this worrisome vision, Celano wrote, came the stigmata: "The marks of the nails began to appear in his hands and feet, just as he had seen them a little before in the crucified man about him. . . . His right side was as though it had been pierced by a lance." (Moses, 182)

This experience at La Verna took place two years before the saint's death, and because he was already quite infirm, it was doubtless the only way for him to react to this latest bellicose initiative. In addition, scholars today surmise that Francis had great concern for his Muslim counterpart al-Kamil, who once again would be the target of this latest Crusade. At La Verna, in a prayer dictated to his confidant, Brother Leo, Francis speaks of God in ways reminiscent of the well-known Islamic ninety-nine names for the Divine. The Qur'an speaks of "the Compassionate, the Merciful, the Sovereign, the Holy, the Peaceful, the Mighty, the Creator, the Forgiver, the Provider, the Generous" (Moses, 182). Francis words are "You are the Most High, You are King of heaven and earth, You are Good, all Good, supreme Good, you are love, wisdom, humility, endurance, rest, peace, beauty, gentleness, Our great consolation, eternal life" (ibid.). These indications that Francis underwent a conversion during his year in Egypt among people of a totally different religious background and his positive relationship with Sultan Malik al-Kamil over the course of that year offer us much food for thought in our own post-9/11 historical reality. It is entirely possible that at some point Francis would have recalled Jesus's instruction: "If you remember that your brother or sister has something against you . . . go and be reconciled" (Matt 5:24).

Malik al-Kamil and his people clearly had something against the Christian Crusaders who were waging war on them. The Christians, under Cardinal Pelagius, consistently rejected overtures toward peace from the Sultan before and during the battle for Damietta. Who exactly, then, was the enemy here? Who should be the one to take a first step toward reconciliation? These are questions directly applicable to our current historical realities.

Following Francis, Following Jesus

9/11

September 11, 2001, stands as one of those watershed moments in individual and national life after which nothing in the United States has felt the same. The horrendous events at the Twin Towers in New York, at the Pentagon in Washington, DC, and in a Pennsylvania field shook the United States and its people to their foundations and produced an outpouring of compassion from the rest of the world toward this country. For a brief historical moment people of good will everywhere joined in mourning the extensive loss of life that day in the United States.

Within days of the 9/11 tragedy a preeminent US scripture scholar, Walter Brueggemann, offered a process for coping with the overwhelming magnitude of this crime. Among Brueggemann's suggestions was the establishment of a period of national mourning as a necessary first step toward individual and collective healing. Significantly, he also urged the United States to ask eventually what in our national life could have provoked such a vicious attack.

Such a wide-ranging examination of conscience in the United States particularly and the West generally could have resulted in the kind of conversion that took place in the life of St. Francis. The Crusades had a clear objective—to retrieve in some form the places in the Middle East considered sacred in Christian history. It was the means used toward this end—war—that Francis found problematic. Likewise, a deeper consideration of the targets in the 9/11 attacks immediately reveals the terrorists' objectives: the global financial power of the West (World Trade Center) and the military reach of the United States and its allies (the Pentagon). Considering carefully and prayerfully these symbols of Western hegemony, as Brueggemann urged, could well have been the first step in a much needed restoration of right relationships on a global scale.

OUR STORIES

Let us start, then, with a kind of personal and communal examination of conscience and move to the larger framework of today's global standoff between West and East.

Consider our stance as people of the rich, industrialized world vis-à-vis sisters and brothers who live in the Middle East, Africa, or the Far East. Do we not have a general sense of superiority or at least a feeling that "they" should or could achieve our standards of ethical and religious values as well as our "God-given freedoms" with some help from us?

Consider our stance as Christians vis-à-vis other faith traditions, particularly Islam. Are we at all aware of the many values those traditions carry; for example, the striking reverence Islam pays to the Holy Mystery we call God, or its dedication to continual prayer and the vital connection between almsgiving and prayer, or its remarkable practice of strict fasting (Ramadan), or the value it places on pilgrimage to its holy city of Mecca? When we consider our own religious practices, can we claim similar fervor and faithfulness?

Consider the many acts of discrimination based on fear directed particularly toward Muslim people living in our neighborhoods, whose very names, manner of dress, physical appearance, and customs remind us of cultures very different from our own and spark feelings of unease and even fear.

Consider today's conflict over immigration policies, particularly in the United States and Europe, wherein the "strangers," particularly from the global South and the East, are too often labeled enemies, threats, usurpers.

Consider and compare with the above a moment when you experienced discrimination on the basis of an unpopular political position; your religion, sex, or sexual orientation; or ethnic background.

SIGNS OF OUR TIMES

"War" on Terrorism

Unfortunately—tragically—the suggestions made by Walter Brueggemann following the attacks on the United States on 9/11 seemed not to make any impact on US leadership or, for that matter, on the US people. It was clear, even as early as the end of that fateful September day, that reprisal would be the principal response, that the United States would take violent revenge on those who had done this monstrous act. And so it was. Before a month had passed the United States declared war against Afghanistan and seventeen months later a second all-out war was launched against Iraq—both military strikes supposedly designed to seek out, stop, and destroy the Islamic militant organization

Al Qaeda, which had taken responsibility for the New York and Washington bombings.

Paradoxically, eight years earlier, in February 1993, a similar but mercifully much less destructive terrorist bombing had taken place at the same World Trade Center in New York. That crime had been successfully dealt with more prudently by the United States. Its perpetrators were sought out by effective police work, charged with the crime, and sentenced in a court of law. But in 2001 no such measured response was contemplated—only revenge, and revenge on a massive scale. From October 7, 2001, the day Afghanistan was attacked by the North Atlantic Treaty Organization, war became the order of the day.

Islamophobia

Equally disturbing has been an almost visceral antagonism toward Islam in the United States specifically, and in Europe as well, since 2001. While it is true that those guilty of the 9/11 massacres were members of Al Qaeda, the broad-based, militant Islamic organization, they did not represent the majority of adherents to the Islamic faith. To be fair, official US statements immediately after the tragedy made this point clearly. Despite the US president's intent to respond in kind to the attacks on New York and Washington, to his credit, he consistently distinguished between Al Qaeda terrorists and faithful followers of Islam. Within a week of 9/11 he visited the Islamic Center in Washington and clearly stated that the acts of violence against innocents at the World Trade Center, the Pentagon, and in Pennsylvania violated the fundamental tenets of the Islamic faith. He also insisted that day on the importance of US citizens understanding this.

Unfortunately, that sentiment failed to permeate public opinion in the United States. Perhaps the crucial distinction between "Islamic extremists"—almost universally used to describe terrorist organizations and actions—and the vast majority of good-willed

Muslims was too subtle or nuanced for our overheated political rhetoric after 9/11. Whatever the reason, it is clear that significant public sentiment in the United States in the post-9/11 world harbors everything from suspicion and antagonism to outright hatred toward anything that resembles Islam.

As noted, the "war against terrorism" has been described as a struggle against "Islamic extremists." This unfortunate coupling of Islam with terrorism has fueled a culture of Islamophobia. Irresponsible statements by public figures have exacerbated that sentiment. To cite just two of these: According to the *New York Times* (December 21, 2011), in a July 2010 speech to the American Enterprise Institute, Newt Gingrich stated categorically that "Sharia law [the law and moral code of Islam] is a moral threat to the survival of freedom in the United States." And *Al Jazeera* (August 19, 2012) reported that US Congressman Joe Walsh (R-Ill.), when asked about Islam at a town hall meeting in 2012, responded, "One thing I'm sure of is that there are people in this country—there is a radical strain of Islam in this country—it's not just over there—trying to kill Americans every week."

Anecdotes abound about acts of discrimination, sometimes quite violent, against people in the United States who seem to have some connection with Islam by reason of their physical appearance, their dress, or their language. Even a cursory search on the Internet reveals study after study of anti-Muslim attitudes and actions in Western countries after 2000 and up to the present.

Enemy Making

Individually and collectively we enable and accept violence against others by first making them into enemies in our minds, or much more subtly, by perceiving them as less worthy or less human than we are.

Our inclination upon encountering people who are different from ourselves, whether individuals, groups, or nations, is not to discover who they are but to classify them, stereotype them, and draw conclusions about them based upon our belief systems. Usually we put others into one of two broad categories—"us" or "them." "Us" consists of people with whom we identify. "Them" are those we consider different. We tend to be biased toward "us."

This dynamic becomes dangerous if we consider "them" not only different but also threatening, hostile, irrelevant, unworthy, or less human than we are. Such perceptions provide moral justification for not allocating resources to "them" and for hurting, ignoring, making scapegoats of, or even killing "them." The psychological process by which we come to believe it unnecessary to treat all people according to the same moral standards is called *moral exclusion.* On a societal level moral exclusion fuels racism, sexism, classism, and war. It is engendered by negative images of "them."

The Christian church in the time of Francis attributed to Muslims many negative images that fueled the fervor against them. Francis undermined this powerful root of enemy making by refusing to accept enemy images of the Sultan and of the Islamic people.

Today, too, exaggerated negative images of Muslims are used to generate public support for warfare or other policies that would seem unacceptable if the public saw the adversary in more real terms.

If possible, do the following social analysis with other people:

• Remember that "enemy making" refers to the dynamic of perceiving others in such a way that it becomes acceptable to hurt, ignore, or kill them. We are not talking about people's intentions toward us. This is not to deny that others actually may have ill intentions toward us, but the issue is how our perception of others might lead us to conflict, oppression, war, or abuse.

- With the above in mind, how does "enemy making" happen? Are we involved? What are the results? Who benefits? Who loses? What can we do to break the habit of enemy making as individuals and as a society?

INVITATION TO RESPOND

We look again at St. Francis. His return from Damietta proved enormously difficult for the saint. Now at the age of thirty-eight (he died at forty-four), his eyesight had begun to fail and his general health was declining. Moreover, after at least a full year away from the brotherhood, he found that they were moving in very different directions from his vision for them. In 1221 Francis wrote another Rule of Life for his brothers to update the so-called Primitive Rule (1209). The Rule of 1221 would ensure that his desire for the Order to be devoted to poverty and peace would outlive him. In it he urged his followers to observe the strictest poverty and to "be subject" (!) to Muslims. Such radical ideas were not politically correct. The final version of the Rule, approved by Pope Honorius III (he of the Fifth and Sixth Crusades) in 1223, eviscerated the bolder aspects of Francis's text, particularly with regard to such revolutionary and "outlandish" ideas as being subject to Muslims (Moses, 178).

Still, Francis stayed the course wherever he could in these final, difficult years, despite the call for yet another Crusade issued by Honorius III in 1224. Francis wrote his eloquent Testament, a kind of last will, in which he recalled that long-ago encounter with the leper and how his revulsion had turned into sweetness of soul and body when he embraced the unfortunate person. He insisted that no one should thwart his vision for the friars, and that it was the Lord who revealed to him the greeting, "May the Lord give you peace."

Again, Francis exemplifies the possibility and importance of dialogue across religious, cultural, and geographic boundaries. Especially in his dramatic dialogue with the Sultan he lived out the sea-crossing texts from chapters 4 and 6 in Mark's Gospel.

These last efforts of the sick and despondent saint to continue the work of reconciliation point to the enormously difficult task of peacemaking. Except for isolated events, such as the local dispute between Assisi's bishop and mayor, Francis did not succeed in any notable way at peace. We can only imagine his consternation upon hearing just two years before his death that another Crusade would be visited on the Christian and Muslim worlds. By this time Francis was acknowledged to be a saint; his efforts with the Sultan were surely widely known. Still, the pope in Rome sought violent solutions to situations that Francis had pointed to and treated as negotiable.

Despite these failures, the Saint of Assisi stands as a preeminent example of the peacemaker. In this, his experience underscores the paradox that lies at the very heart of Christ's message: "the one who would lose his or her life for my sake will gain it"; "unless the grain of wheat falls into the ground and dies, it remains just a grain of wheat"; "let both [the weeds and the wheat] grow together until the harvest"; "from that time on, Jesus began to show his disciples that he must go to Jerusalem and undergo great suffering at the hands of the elders and chief priests and scribes, and be killed—and on the third day be raised."

This enormous paradox in the life of Christ, reflected in the life of Francis, brings us to our response. It is at once clear and enormously difficult. For we are faced with a global problem—the growing standoff between an increasingly secularized Western industrialized world and the East of Islam older religious traditions and vast populations, exasperated to the point of despair by the patent contradictions in Western rhetoric and practice. What sort of response can one possibly offer to this vast chasm?

The great liberation theologian Gustavo Gutiérrez often said that the best action is a good theory. He also put the same idea another way: we all need a utopia, a vision, some overarching ideal to help us imagine totally new possibilities. It seems that Francis of Assisi, especially in his great dream of forestalling a war between the Christian and Muslim worlds of his time, provides our historical moment with just such a utopia. We in the West have the opportunity to follow Jesus's injunction to go and be reconciled with the sister or brother who has something against us. We in the West have sinned in many ways against our sisters and brothers in the East—just think of Afghanistan, Iraq, drones, regime change, oil, our way of life. Those sisters and brothers have much against us. We can well ask again, as we could have in the thirteenth century when the Christian West (the church) ignored overtures of peace from the Muslim East—who exactly is the enemy here? Francis encountered a similar situation as he became familiar with the details of the Crusades and with the "other," Malik al-Kamil. He recognized immense good will in the church's supposed adversaries.

Could this motivate people of good will today at every level of life: interpersonal, regional, national, and international? What consequences could follow a sincere overture of dialogue, friendship, nonviolence, and understanding between ourselves and our Islamic sisters and brothers today?

If possible, do the following exercise with other people:

Think of a nation or group that our government perceives as enemy, portrays as enemy, and approaches as enemy. Recall the words and example of Christ regarding an enemy. Take a moment to hear Christ's words and example as an invitation to accept the power of the Spirit.

• Learning from Francis, what could you do to plead for the violence against this so-called enemy to stop? to approach this enemy unarmed? to show brotherly or sisterly love toward this enemy?

• What economic gains do you reap from your nation's violence? What could you do to refuse those economic benefits? How could you get to know so-called enemies enough to learn from them?

Dare to commit yourself to some or all of these actions, remembering that you are empowered by the Spirit to love in ways not considered humanly possible.

7

Francis and Suffering

Dialogue with the Crucified and Risen One

He called the crowd with his disciples, and said to them, "If any want to become my followers, let them deny themselves and take up their cross and follow me. For those who want to save their life will lose it, and those who lose their life for my sake, and for the sake of the gospel, will save it. For what will it profit them to gain the whole world and forfeit their life?" (Mark 8:34–36)

While we live we are constantly being delivered to death for Jesus's sake, so that the life of Jesus may be revealed in our mortal flesh. Death is at work in us, but life in you. (2 Cor 4:11–12)

FRANCIS'S STORY

In September 1224, two years before his death, after a period of intense activity, Francis made a retreat at a place called Mt. Alverna. There on a rugged cliffside of this lonely mountain he entered into a forty-day period of fasting, solitude, and prayer. In this poverty Francis received an inpouring of the Spirit such as he had never known before. As Francis read the gospel account of Christ's passion, he experienced an unquenchable desire to be with Christ in his suffering. As he continued in prayer, Francis realized that what he longed for was to be given to him in a very mysterious way. The following account describes the revelation that he received just before the wounds of Christ, the stigmata, appeared in his hands, feet, and side.

The next day came, that is, the Feast of the Cross. And St. Francis, sometime before dawn, began to pray outside the entrance of his cell, turning his face toward the east. And he prayed in this way: "My Lord Jesus Christ, I pray you to grant me two graces before I die: the first is that during my life I may feel in my soul and in my body, as much as possible, that pain which You, dear Jesus, sustained in the hour of Your most bitter passion. The second is that I may feel in my heart, as much as possible, that excessive love with which You, O Son of God, were inflamed in willingly enduring such suffering for us sinners."

And remaining for a long time in that prayer, he understood that God would grant it to him, and that it would soon be conceded to him to feel those things as much as is possible for a mere creature.

Having received this promise, St. Francis began to contemplate with intense devotion the Passion of Christ and His infinite charity. And the fervor of his devotion increased so much within him that he utterly transformed himself into Jesus through love and compassion. And while he was thus inflaming himself in this contemplation, on that same morning he saw coming down from heaven a seraph with six resplendent and flaming wings. As the seraph, flying swiftly, came closer to St. Francis, so that he could perceive him clearly, he noticed that He had the likeness of a crucified man, and his wings were so disposed that two wings attended above His head, two were spread out to fly, and the other two covered his entire body.

On seeing this, St. Francis was very much afraid, and at the same time he was filled with joy and grief and amazement. He felt intense joy from the friendly look of Christ, who appeared to him in a very familiar way and gazed at him very kindly. But on the other hand, seeing Him nailed to the cross, he felt boundless grief and compassion. Next, he was greatly amazed at such an astounding and extraordinary vision, for he knew well that the affliction of suffering is not in accord with the immortality of the angelic seraph. And while he was marveling thus, He who was appearing to him revealed to him that this vision was shown to him by Divine Providence in this particular form in order that he should understand that he was to be utterly transformed into the direct likeness of Christ Crucified, not by physical martyrdom, but by enkindling of the mind. (Brown, 190–91)

Perhaps of all the stories of Francis that we have considered, it is the account of Francis on Mt. Alverna that is most difficult for our modern sensibilities. Any initial skepticism about the historicity of this story makes it easier for us to dismiss this as the stuff of medieval legend. And yet, it is hard for the most critical historian to dispute the testimony of friars who saw the wounds on Francis in spite of his efforts to conceal them. Do we not know from our own experience that the mind is intimately related to the body? Is it then impossible for an interior state, lived more and more intensely over a lifetime, to manifest itself in the exterior body?

It is not the intention here to convince anyone of the historicity of the stigmata. Everyone must interpret the truth of this story for himself or herself. Our real problem may come at another level, when we are tempted to dismiss the story of the stigmata as just another example of medieval asceticism and piety that we find unhealthy and grossly negative. Doesn't this story of the stigmata of Francis glorify suffering in a way that seems inappropriate to us today?

The modern religious attitude toward suffering is fundamentally different from that in the time of Francis. Suffering is not understood as necessary for salvation or as deserved because of original sin. Furthermore, so much suffering in the world neither ennobles those who suffer nor contributes anything positive to their existence. But with all these theological and ethical reservations aside, how do we come to terms with suffering in our lives and in our world? More specifically, what is the relationship between our faith and the suffering that we feel and see all around us? Does Francis have anything to teach us about a faithful and transforming response to suffering?

Before we return to the story of Francis on Mt. Alverna, let us look at his response to suffering over the context of a lifetime. In what ways did Francis know suffering? What consequences did it have for him? What meaning was he able to draw from these experiences? What can we learn from the ways in which suffering was present in the life of Francis and how he responded to it?

Suffering and the Conversion of Francis

As a young man in the prime of his life, Francis experienced firsthand the shattering realities of warfare, imprisonment, and debilitating sickness. These experiences undoubtedly contributed to the profound crisis in his life that led to his conversion. Through these very painful experiences the world of Francis was "cracked open" and his ego broken, so that something new could be born.

As we considered in Chapter 1, the movement of his conversion carried Francis from the point of finding the suffering of a leper utterly repulsive to the point at which he could embrace the leper and offer care and support. Francis no longer feared but embraced the physical and emotional suffering of the most marginalized of his society. His experience of the world was enlarged to include that which had formerly been rejected and shunned. And in the context of this new enlarged worldview, the suffering leper was no longer repulsive but "sweet" to his inner heart. Clearly, a transformation had begun to occur. Francis teaches us that human suffering may be the occasion for a transforming moment of conversion. Experiences of suffering have the potential to open us to a new understanding of ourselves and God. Suffering can sensitize us to the pain of the world. Our experiences of suffering can link us to larger communities of suffering and support of which we have been largely unaware, energizing us for struggle and advocacy on fronts that have become very personal.

The painful alienation that Francis felt in relation to his family, especially his father, grew until these relationships reached a breaking point in that dramatic moment in the cathedral courtyard of Assisi. When Francis stood naked before the bishop, his family, and all of the townspeople, he removed himself from the security of family and community. Jesus taught this same lesson in a number of those "hard sayings" directed at those who would follow him (for example, "Leave father and mother behind," and "Let the dead bury the dead"). He experienced painful rejection from his hometown when he returned to preach in the synagogue of Nazareth. How many of us have known painful alienation from our family of origin or our hometown or ethnic community because we have sought to be faithful to a different path?

In Chapter 2 we considered how Francis relinquished any claim to protection, status, shelter, and livelihood that his family could provide him. Francis moved from his former life at the center of a walled city to a life outside the walls, vulnerable to the painful inequities of the poorest of the poor. For Francis and for Clare the invitation to discipleship meant the willingness to risk alienation from their community. It meant the willingness to become insecure and vulnerable to suffering. The call to conversion meant, fundamentally, a willingness to relinquish all claims on their former life.

Francis and his brothers and sisters willingly and joyfully embraced the physical hardship and suffering that the poor of that time experienced involuntarily at the margins of social existence. Fundamental to their mission in the world as followers of Christ was this compassionate solidarity with the marginalized. Wearing only coarse tunics on their backs and living most of the time in what amounted to lean-tos made of sticks and brush, Francis and his brothers knew the discomforts of nature as the most marginalized in their society must have known them. They knew the hardships of inadequate shelter that barely shielded them from the cold of winter or the heat of summer. They knew the backbreaking labor of the peasants working the fields. They knew the gnawing emptiness of hunger of those who eked out an existence from day to day. This was a conscious choice, an intentional pastoral strategy that was radically rooted in the witness of the historical Jesus and in the discipleship journey that ends and begins anew at the foot of the cross. They bore in their bodies and souls the suffering of the poor, believing that they were bearing the suffering Christ.

But the original Franciscan community was not a collection of individuals all demonstrating tremendous feats of ascetic self-denial. Rather, it was a community seeking to be faithful to a call to live on the margins and intent on helping its members to be faithful to that difficult mission. This may be the most important aspect of the Franciscan witness of suffering. Francis himself was not an ascetic superman able to endure all suffering by the sheer force of his spirituality.

It was his friend and sister Clare who so often sustained him through the most difficult and painful moments of his life. Their intimacy and constant love for each other enabled Francis to endure extremely difficult crises of vision and leadership within the

Order. In those years when his health began to fail him, Francis sought out the company and solace of Clare, who nurtured him through the physical agonies of the last year before his death.

This deep tenderness in the relationship between Francis and Clare characterized the quality of life of the Franciscan community in the relations of all the brothers and sisters. Their community was one in which each member bore the burdens of the others, a community whose members ministered to one another in sickness, trial, and want.

Francis and Bodily Suffering

Toward the end of his life Francis was racked with pain from a very serious eye disease that threatened his sight and made ordinary sunlight an unbearable torment. On one occasion his brothers persuaded him to avail himself of the best medical remedies of that day. Unfortunately, medical opinion was that cauterization of the temples would relieve the agonizing pain that Francis experienced in his eyes. As the doctor prepared the hot iron to cauterize his temples in what would be an excruciating procedure, Francis pleaded with Brother Fire to be gentle with him. And it is reported by witnesses and by Francis himself that when the operation was performed, he felt no pain. Francis was one who could dialogue with his pain, talking to it not as an enemy but as if it were a brother or sister.

When his deteriorating health finally brought Francis to the point of death, he composed the last stanza of the Canticle:

> All praise be yours, my Lord, through Sister
> Death,
> from whose embrace no mortal can escape.

From these lines, sung by the brothers in those last hours, we see that Francis was able to greet and welcome even death as a sister.

He embraced the end of his life as something to be celebrated rather than feared. Elias, the friar who would replace Francis as the leader of the Order, rebuked Francis at the hour of his death for singing rather than saying prayers of confession and mourning. But Francis kept on singing for joy. As death drew near, Francis requested that the brothers lay him naked on the ground in imitation of Christ and in his desire to be close to the earth. For Francis, even death was a joyous occasion.

Francis and the Suffering of the Cross

The life of St. Francis has much to teach us about how to integrate the suffering that comes to us as fragile creatures. Like any human being, Francis knew the pain resulting from conflict and injustice, sickness, accident, aging, and death. But the suffering that Francis knew on Mt. Alverna transcended these experiences of suffering because it was born of a conscious choice to embrace with his whole being the suffering and the love of the crucified Christ. The gift of the stigmata was not simply a miracle given near the end of Francis's life. It was rather the fruit of his whole faith journey, the culminating moment of an entire lifetime of striving to identify more and more with the crucified Christ. Francis sought to make his very existence cruciform by drawing more and more of his life and experience into the reality of the cross. It was finally on Mt. Alverna that this intention manifested itself physically in his body in the wounds of the crucified Christ.

We reflect again on the prayer that shaped Francis's experience on Mt. Alverna:

> *My Lord Jesus Christ, I pray you to grant me two graces before I die: the first is that during my life I may feel in my soul and in my body, as much as possible, that pain which You, dear Jesus, sustained in the hour of Your most bitter passion. The second is that I may feel in my heart as much*

*as possible, that excessive love with which You, O Son of
God, were inflamed in willingly enduring such suffering
for us sinners.*

On Mt. Alverna, Francis prayed that his heart might be opened
to compassionate solidarity so that he could feel the suffering of
Christ on the cross as well as the love that motivated Christ to
endure that pain.

At the core of Franciscan spirituality is this striving to enter
into the divine heart to feel the pathos of suffering love that
God feels for the world. Francis's striving to identify with the
crucified Christ was not meant to be a spiritual absorption into
suffering for its own sake and should not be construed as a mas-
ochistic sanctification of pain. Rather, Francis sought to know
God by abiding with God in the passion. Francis embodied and
illuminated the words of St. Paul, who wrote: "In my flesh I am
completing what is lacking in Christ's afflictions" (Col 1:24).
Francis believed that if we claim to be the body of Christ, we
are called to participate in the suffering, death, and resurrection
of Jesus. We are called to die and be raised again in new life, not
just at the end of our life but in each moment of our discipleship
journey. Francis accompanies us in following Jesus in the way
of the cross, the way of active love on behalf of the crucified of
the world.

FOLLOWING FRANCIS, FOLLOWING JESUS

The Scandal of the Cross

Francis points beyond himself to the gospel story and asks us
our response to the cross of Christ. Here we reach a fundamental
problem: the scandal of the crucified God. Jesus died in what
seemed to be a complete rupture from his own mission, from

his community, and ultimately from his God. Jesus, the one who proclaimed the nearness of God, whom he knew as Abba Father, was hung on the cross, seemingly abandoned by God. The gospel message of the cross is a scandal and stumbling block because it does not bring us the message of success or the triumphant power of goodness, but rather of God's presence hidden in what is defeat, loss, abandonment, and death. How is it that the divine Being is revealed in the agony of a crucifixion?

As the original discipleship community experienced a profound crisis in the loss of their leader and in the manner of his death, so the first generations of the church were faced with the difficulty of interpreting to the world they sought to evangelize how the death of Jesus could mean anything other than the disastrous end of an obscure messianic movement in a remote corner of the Roman Empire. In just what sense was there "good news" to be found in the death of one denounced as a blasphemer by the religious establishment of his society and executed as a political revolutionary by the imperial power of the Roman state?

The church was tempted to resolve this problem by removing the scandal of the cross. We see this temptation reflected in the Gospels themselves. As Mark is considered the most original, its perspective on the crucifixion is the most stark. Mark's Jesus cries out from the cross, "My God, my God, why hast thou forsaken me?" For Mark, the way of the cross, the way of solidarity and resistance, is the historical paradigm for the discipleship journey, the path that any disciple of Jesus must be prepared to follow. Luke's account, much later than Mark's, tones down the death of Jesus by transforming the crucified One into a confident martyr, obedient to divine necessity. And in the Gospel of John, Jesus becomes the exalted One orchestrating the final events of his earthly life before he ascends into heaven.

Throughout the history of the church this temptation to remove the historical scandal of the crucifixion has resulted in theologies of the cross that provide doctrinal explanations of why the cross had to be and why it makes perfect sense. The cross has been interpreted solely as a symbol of divine forgiveness for the individual rather than as the cost of discipleship and the ultimate example of active nonviolence. The church has softened the scandal by separating the cross of Jesus from the historical path that led to it. The historical path of the cross led Jesus to the margins of his society in loving solidarity with the outcast and into an ever-deepening conflict with the authorities for their maintenance of systems that exclude and dominate. This path would ultimately lead Jesus through the horrific night of betrayal and desertion, through trial, torture, and execution.

We must not give in to this temptation to remove the scandal of the cross of Jesus. The cross is not meant to provide neat answers to our inquiry about the nature of God, nor does it provide easy images of divine wisdom. Rather, the cross reveals the inadequacy of human knowledge to comprehend the ways of God. The cross challenges the assumption that human knowledge is able to understand God at all. And so the cross is scandal and folly to human reason. In the same way the cross directly challenges human strength and power. Far from revealing an omnipotent God wielding power from heaven, the cross reveals a God hidden in the profoundly negative depths of history, the garbage dump called Golgotha. God is revealed in weakness rather than strength, in failure rather than success.

The cross radically undercuts the standards of the world, exposing how the divine gifts of human power and intelligence are easily coopted by evil and for the purposes of oppression. The cross is a challenge that goes to the very foundation of human reason and power by asking: Are human reason and power the instruments of oppression and violence or of justice and liberation? The cross of Jesus exposes human reason and power as false gods, whenever they claim for themselves an absolute authority. Any time that human power or reason is used to carry out or justify oppression, these human potentialities declare themselves to be in open rebellion against the reign of God.

The message of the gospel was a scandal to the Jews and a stumbling block to the Greeks because of the claim that God is revealed in the form of one hanging from a cross. The gospel message says that on the cross God is crucified, making clear to every generation the foolishness of God in the face of human reason. The cross is folly and continues to be a stumbling block when it is not glossed over into a more palatable religious symbol. And so we ask ourselves again: What meaning do we find in this event of the cross, the death of Jesus? In what sense does God suffer for us and for our world in the crucifixion of Jesus of Nazareth? What does the crucified Christ teach us about the power of nonviolence and about the cost of following Jesus?

The Scandal of the World's Suffering

Poverty in the world is a scandal. In a world where there is so much wealth, so many resources to feed everyone, it is unfathomable that there are so many hungry children, that there are so many children without an education, so many poor persons. (Pope Francis, Meeting with Students of Jesuit Schools, June 7, 2013)

If we are able to view the cross of Jesus without removing the scandal of the crucifixion, we are more likely to face without rationalization or denial the scandal of the world's suffering. Any theology of the cross that does not help us to see and address this scandal is irrelevant and inappropriate. An authentic theology of the cross must enable us to face the scandal of the unspeakable suffering of millions of people who are afflicted with violence and marginalized by poverty and injustice. And so it is the scandal of the cross borne by the vast majority of the world that provides an urgent context for our reflection as we ask the question: What does the cross say to the suffering of those who are oppressed, hungry, homeless, and abandoned? What does the cross say to the suffering of earth?

This question is best answered by those who actually suffer, especially by the faithful who occupy the margins of society. The authors of this book have had the privilege of being with peoples of the global South in countries like South Sudan and Nicaragua, Cambodia and El Salvador, South Africa and Honduras, the Philippines and Guatemala, Peru, Iraq, Palestine, and Bolivia. The suffering of the people in these countries has been bitter, longstanding, and immense.

For millions of people throughout the world, the experience of suffering has been an excruciating barrier to a humane existence. There is no way to say that this suffering has somehow ennobled or purified impoverished people on the margins of our world. There is no way to say that the suffering of earth is according to the will of God. We must resist the temptation to remove the scandal and offense of this suffering with any romantic distortion. This suffering is an abomination rooted in systemic injustice and greed. It is an absolute contradiction to the will of God.

But in the midst of this history of suffering many communities of faith in Latin America, South Africa, Palestine, the Philippines, and elsewhere have been able to approach the mystery and the scandal of the cross with an intuitive understanding rooted in their own context and struggle. In Christ crucified they have seen the God who is in complete and absolute solidarity with all the crucified of the world. This divine love embraces the crucified ones of the world in order to transform their condition: to alleviate their pain, to heal their wounds, to walk with them in the struggle to transform situations of injustice and oppression. The God revealed in Jesus does not go about this liberating work from afar but from within history, in the very midst of death, even from the cross. As long as anyone continues to suffer from poverty, war, oppression, and other forms of destructive violence, God continues to hang on the cross.

Discipleship Journey Is the Way of the Cross

Out of this history of suffering, many faithful communities, aware of being accompanied by the God of love, have been able to rise up, shoulder their own crosses, and follow Jesus in the way of his passion. By taking action to resist evil and the causes of suffering, they began to enter ever more deeply into the reality of the cross. Such Christians are part of a long tradition in the history of the church, a tradition of fools like Francis, whose passionate identification with the crucified Christ has led them into radical commitments on behalf of a suffering world.

In Jesus, Peter, and Paul; in Franz Jägerstätter and Edith Stein; in Rutilio Grande and Jean Donovan; in Steve Biko and Chico Mendes; in the Cambodian martyrs, Jerry Popieluszko, and the martyrs of Argentina's dirty war; in Enrique Angelleli and Juan Gerardi, in Frans Van der Lught, and in countless others, we honor this long tradition of prophets who endured suffering in order to speak the truth, who proclaimed hope in the inbreaking of justice and peace in the midst of injustice and conflict. We honor these "fools" who have defended life and who refused to be chased away by forces that threatened them with death, these "fools" who followed Jesus in the "via negativa," the way of the cross.

The call to take up the cross of Christ is the invitation to be in solidarity with the crucified of the world and to die with Christ in order to bring about the New Creation. The cross confronts us with a question about our own willingness to enter more deeply into union with God's suffering love for a broken world. We are called to embrace the struggle of the crucified of the world, to suffer if need be in solidarity with and alongside people who are poor and marginalized. The followers of Jesus can expect persecutions precisely because of our resistance to conditions that violate human dignity.

This invitation is as difficult to respond to now as it has always been. In every generation the response entails contradicting enormous religious, political, economic, and social forces. Today, it means embracing those who are marginalized in compassionate solidarity as brother or sister and resisting with all one's being the causes of their suffering. Compassionate solidarity means struggling against "powers and principalities," political and economic systems that shape the world and cause the suffering of millions of our brothers and sisters. Compassionate solidarity means struggling to resist and transform the systems that bring harm and pain and to change them into systems that can mediate justice and community.

Do we not fear for the soul of the church in the First World, when something so central to the gospel message, "Take up your cross and follow me," is so little practiced? When the first-world church contemplates the cross, for the most part it sees only an innocuous icon totally divorced from the painful historical reality. We have effectively eliminated the scandal of the cross by separating the cross of Jesus from the historical path that led to it, the path we are called to follow as disciples of Christ. We have sought to circumvent the cross and go directly to the good news of the resurrection. We have sought out a religious faith that eliminates the costs of discipleship and numbs us to the suffering of the world. If we cannot face the scandal of the cross of Jesus, we will not be able to face the scandal of the unjust suffering of millions in human history and in our world today.

If we were to truly open our eyes and "see with eyes that see," we would no longer be able to avoid the great ocean of human suffering throughout history up to our own time. The human soul understandably recoils from such a horrible vision of pain. This vision strikes us in the core of our being and in deep places of personal pain. We shrink back in ignorance because the mind cannot grasp; in indifference because the will cannot respond; in numbness because the emotions collapse. If we truly open our life and our heart to the suffering of God in the world, won't we be immediately paralyzed, overwhelmed by the immensity of it? What kind of spirituality will make it possible to open ourselves to the divine heart and to abide with God in suffering love for the world?

A Spirituality of the Cross

A spirituality of the cross begins to emerge wherever people of faith become aware that nothing can separate us from the love of God. A loving God is present in the midst of our suffering. But a spirituality based on the cross means far more than the acceptance of sadness and life's inevitable hardships.

A spirituality based on the cross must ultimately mean following the historical path that for Jesus led to the cross. In following Jesus we bear the cross in our resistance to sin, both personal and collective. We bear the cross in our willingness to confront the idolatrous claims sometimes made by human reason and power. We proclaim what is foolishness in the face of human ideology. We proclaim what is weakness in the face of human power and the will to oppress.

True identification with the crucified One as experienced by Francis will not take place in the abstract as a religious ideal or by way of good intentions. This identification with the crucified One is authentically realized by following Jesus's way of the cross. But this gospel invitation does not demand directly that we suffer; rather, it calls us to love, which, because of evil, will mean suffering.

Here it is important to return to Mt. Alverna, where Francis sought to know God by abiding with Jesus in his passion. Had the revelation on Mt. Alverna been an isolated event, divorced from the context of Francis's life, its witness for us would be suspect and severely limited. The giving of the stigmata would be only a mystical glorification of suffering. But from Mt. Alverna we can look back with Francis over his entire lifetime to see the path of discipleship that he sought to follow. In this way, we understand that a truly Franciscan spirituality is not so much a mysticism of suffering as it is a spirituality of following Jesus. Francis teaches us how we can take up our own cross and walk the path of our discipleship journey. He teaches us that the way of the cross is a never-ending process of conversion, of dying and rising to new life. We must find ways to deepen this conversion of eyes, ears, and heart so that we are able to recognize the crucified Christ in the face of the leper.

We must find ways to dispel the psychic numbness that stifles our compassion and to unlock the untapped capacity for love in our hearts. In faithful community we can gather the courage needed to face conflicts with our families and our society when the call to discipleship leads us along a different path. In community we receive and give the support that is necessary if we are to be faithful to our mission.

With each step along this path and with Francis as our companion we find ourselves more willing to relinquish the absolute claim on our lives and increasingly able to let go of those things that may insulate us from the suffering of the world. We walk with Francis step by difficult step toward the margins, where we encounter and enter places of suffering. There we may experience many emotions: fear, revulsion, hurt, anger, love. Our fear gradually decreases as we learn to dialogue with those who suffer and with our own pain; we learn again how to care for others and how to be cared for; we begin to learn what it means to accompany someone in his or her struggle and to be accompanied in ours. We find that we are more willing to risk ourselves not out of self-destructiveness but because of our compassionate identification with others who suffer.

As we probe the deeper causes of unjust suffering in our world, we take up the struggle against mammoth structures that inflict suffering. We do this with a hope that is not rooted in our own efforts or dependent on the expectation of success. We confront radical evil as if our efforts can make a difference. Here the grace of the stigmata may be given to faithful individuals and communities who are seeking to enter more deeply into the pain of the world. These individuals and communities bear in their lives the wounds of Christ as they are asked to suffer with the people. Our mutual solidarity with others begins to teach us about the oneness of the human family, indeed the oneness of creation. From Mt. Alverna we hear the cries of all creation expressed in that cry of one hanging from the cross. And we know that we are not alone. We know that our suffering is God's, and that nothing in life or in death can separate us from the love of God.

From Mt. Alverna we stand with Francis in contemplation of the cross of compassionate solidarity. We pray that our hearts will be filled with the love for which Christ died on the cross for the people of God, for it is to this death that we are called, to die and be raised new women and men who struggle and hope for a new world. From Mt. Alverna we see with Francis the vision of a time when the scandalous suffering of the people, indeed the suffering of all creation, will be embraced in healing love and death will be overthrown, encompassed by transforming life. From Mt. Alverna we recognize that mysterious joining of suffering and joy in the compassionate heart that cannot be analyzed or even adequately described. We catch a glimpse of this grace in the life of Francis. The presence of joy in the midst of struggle and suffering is the most mature fruit of the Christian life, a sure sign of the working of the Spirit. This joy is also a seed of promise that points toward the glorious future to which we are all called, when God will be all in all.

We began this reflection with a story of Francis on Mt. Alverna; we close with the story of a Franciscan in the twentieth century who in April 1945 was one of several thousand captives jammed into a freight train moving through Germany. As the Allied armies penetrated deeper and deeper into Germany, the Nazi SS herded the survivors of the concentration camp Buchenwald onto a train headed for some unknown place. Among these wretched souls from all social classes and nationalities was a small band of Franciscans. For endless days those passengers on this death train descended into a hell of torment as they experienced the suffering of hunger, exposure, violence, and radical evil. One of the Franciscans wrote of that experience:

These extremities of suffering plunge us into acute anxiety. It is no longer simply the anxiety that grips any living thing as death approaches. Amid our terrible distress there arises in us a strange feeling that eats away at those inmost certainties which till now had sustained us. We have a growing impression that we have been handed over to some blind, savage power. There we are, thousands of men abandoned to hunger, cold, vermin, and death. The human being is completely crushed. Man, whom we had till now believed was made in God's image, now seems laughable: worthless, helpless, hopeless; a being caught up in a whirlwind of forces that play with him, or rather, pay absolutely no attention to him. Among the corpses that lie in the water of the car, eyes turned back, is a companion or a friend. Everything we can see, every experience we must undergo, tells us we are in the grip of an iron law, handed over to the play of blind forces—and that this, and this alone, is reality. . . .

Black night fills our souls. And yet, on the morning of April 26 when one of us is in his last moments and the light has almost left his eyes, what rises from our hearts to our lips is not a cry of despair or rebellion, but a song, a song of praise: Francis of Assisi's Canticle of Brother Sun! Nor

*do we have to force ourselves to sing it. It rises spontane-
ously out of our darkness and nakedness, as though it were
the only language fit for such a moment.*

*What brings us in such circumstances to praise God
for and through the great cosmic brotherhood? Theories
have no place in our utter confusion of spirit; they offer no
shelter against the storm. The only thing that remains and
is priceless in our eyes is the patience and friendship this
or that comrade shows you. Such an act by someone who,
like yourself, is immersed in suffering and anxiety, is a ray
of light that falls miraculously into the wretched darkness
that envelops us. It re-creates you, makes you a human being once again. (Leclerc, 233–34)*

*They say that after the horrors of Auschwitz someone asked
with understandable indignation, "Where was God?"
Someone else answered with unguarded serenity: "God
was in Auschwitz." (Sobrino 2004, 146)*

Our Stories

Reflect on times or places of pain in your life.

• Did anyone accompany you through this time? Have you
come to know yourself in a different way through these times of
suffering? Have you come to know God in a new way? Was that
time of suffering in your life ultimately humanizing or dehumanizing? Did that experience of suffering introduce you into a larger
community of suffering that you had been unaware of prior to
your own experience?

• Describe a time in which you encountered the suffering of
another. What was the nature of that suffering, and how did it

affect you? Did it open emotional space within you or close you down? What was your response, and why do you think you responded in that way?

• What has your family or faith community taught you about the way to deal with suffering in your life? in the world? How has your understanding of suffering evolved through your life experience? Does your faith shape your response to the experience of suffering?

• Have you ever experienced rejection or revilement for a condition over which you had no control? How did you respond to this? What effects did it have on you?

• Have you ever suffered pain for a decision that you made on moral grounds? What did that feel like to you? How did you respond?

SIGNS OF OUR TIMES

It is difficult to know for sure in what sense Francis may have tried to move beyond compassion to change the social structures and systems that create suffering. The one who preached a sermon simply by walking silently through the streets of Assisi undoubtedly understood that actions proclaim a message. His life at the margins was in itself a prophetic witness. Like Jesus, Francis made a political statement by locating himself with the poor and marginalized.

The question is one of the church's own self-image as it ministers to the world. For so many generations we have understood our mission in the world as charity to the poor. We have analyzed the problem of the suffering of the poor as something that we, the "haves," can ameliorate by generous redistribution of resources. As we begin to regard our faith in a more global context, we come to a much more profound understanding of the sources of the suffering of the poor.

Aware as no other generation before us, we see on the nightly news, in the morning newspaper, and all over the Internet and social media the suffering sea of humanity across the world. We are coming to understand that all the people of the earth share an interdependent web of financial and natural resources, economic and political relationships, and that we humans are, in fact, intrinsically interconnected with the rest of the cosmos. We see that the very systems that provide our wealth and over-consumption impoverish others. We may be shocked to find that international trade agreements, wage structures, investment processes, and a host of other public policies and practices benefit us while exploiting multitudes of other people.

The following reflection helps us to look at how we move from solidarity with the marginalized to confrontation with systems.

Let us revisit the parable of the Good Samaritan, which has become for many in the church a very important ethical foundation for social action. The hero finds someone bloodied and beaten, lying in a ditch, near death. Unlike others, who pass by the victim unmoved, the good Samaritan responds with compassion by taking the victim to an inn and paying for his medical care and upkeep. If on his next trip the Samaritan were to encounter yet another person in the ditch, we hope that his compassionate response would be the same. But how many times would this happen before the Samaritan began to ask why this was happening? Perhaps he would realize that the truly compassionate act is to find out what situations are creating so many victims.

His compassion would take the form of an inquiry: Why are there bandits along this road? How can they be stopped from this violence? What can be done to give the bandits themselves alternatives to violence? The good Samaritan would be, in fact, engaging in a form of social analysis.

This is the challenge to compassionate people everywhere as we encounter in the ditch the victims of society. There is an obvious urgency to respond to the immediate needs of the person lying in the ditch. And we must. To provide water for migrants and refugees crossing the desert in Arizona; to find shelter for homeless families in Washington, DC; to provide nutritious meals for hungry children in Appalachia; to care for those who are suffering—is to do the work of the gospel. But eventually, if our compassion is to be effective, we must ask ourselves Why? Why is this happening? What are the conditions that create victims? What are the political, economic, cultural, and ecological systems that define and affect this situation of suffering? How might our lives be benefitting from systems that impoverish or exploit other people around the globe?

INVITATION TO RESPOND

Reflect on one experience of suffering that you have encountered. This experience of suffering has had an impact on your life or on persons for whom you care. It has also been brought about by recognizable social or environmental injustice. Let your compassion for the concrete person in the ditch take the shape of an inquiry as you probe to find out how and why this suffering happens and who may benefit from it. Take time for a serious social analysis:

1. Who are the losers in this situation? Are there winners?
2. Look behind the immediate circumstances of the victim and his or her suffering and consider the larger political, economic, cultural, and environmental conditions that shape this experience. Analyze which systems contribute to this suffering and which minimize it. For example, what are some of the root causes of migration (war,

street violence, poverty, job loss, climate change)? Why are families homeless in Washington, DC (underemployment, inadequate minimum wage, lack of affordable housing, racism)? Why are so many children in Appalachia hungry (unemployment, environmental destruction, inadequate education, or substandard health care)?

3. What kinds of systemic change are needed to alleviate this suffering? How can you join others to promote sustainable peace, fair trade, just employment policies and practices, right relationships with the rest of creation? How can you promote racial justice, gender equality, and respect for diversity?

Allow your compassion and your anger to reenter the situation and move you to respond.

8

Francis and Contemplation

Dialogue with the Spirit

When I look at your heavens, the work of your fingers, the moon and the stars that you have established; what are human beings that you are mindful of them, mortals that you care for them? Yet you have made them a little lower than God, and crowned them with glory and honor. (Psalm 8:3–5)

FRANCIS'S STORY

Francis would often pray a simple prayer: Who are you, God, and who am I? To contemplate the Creator of the cosmos is also to seek to know our own place in that creation. On the one hand, we are born into this world trailing wisps of divine glory; on the other, we are nothing but grass that fades, creatures made of dust. Who are you, God, and who am I? Living in this paradox is the contemplative's essential challenge. Francis knew it well.

For who could ever express the height of the affection by which he was carried away as concerning all the things that are God's? Who could tell the sweetness which he enjoyed in contemplating in His creatures the wisdom, power and goodness of the Creator? Truly such thoughts often filled him with wondrous and unspeakable joy as he beheld the sun, or raised his eyes to the moon, or gazed on the stars, and the firmament. O simple piety! O pious simplicity! Even towards little worms he glowed with exceeding love, because he had read that word concerning the Savior, "I am a worm, and no man." Wherefore he used to pick them up in the way and put them in a safe place, that they might not be crushed by the feet of passersby. What shall I say of other lower creatures, when in winter he would cause honey or the best wine to be provided for bees, that they might not perish from cold?

. . .

What gladness do you think the beauty of flowers afforded to his mind as he observed the grace of their form and perceived the sweetness of their perfume? For he turned forthwith the eye of consideration to the beauty of that Flower which, brightly coming forth in springtime from the root of Jesse, has by its perfume raised up countless thousands of the dead. And when he came upon a quantity of flowers he would preach to them and invite them to praise the Lord, just as if they had been gifted with reason. So also cornfields, and vineyards, stones, woods, and all the beauties of the field, fountains of waters, all the verdure of gardens, earth, and fire, air and wind would he with sincerest purity exhort to the love and willing service of God. In short he called all creatures by the name of brother, and in a surpassing manner, of which other men had no experience, he discerned the hidden things of creation with the eye of the heart, as one who had already escaped into the glorious liberty of the children of God. Now, O good Jesus, in the heavens with the angels he is praising You as *admirable who when on earth did surely preach You to all creatures as lovable. (Celano, First Life, nos. 80, 81)*

The Canticle of Creation, composed so near the end of Francis's life, when he was physically suffering and emotionally drained, offers a glimpse into the soul of a man whose whole being was drawn to contemplate the divine mirrored in the reality of life around him.

Thus was the spirituality of the saint of Assisi defined. His way of being was that of profound contemplation: contemplation viewed not as withdrawal from the world, but as entry into its deepest gift—the mystery of life, the presence of God in life and mirrored by life. He moved through life in contemplation, in a fundamental attitude of receptiveness to the Spirit and a primary attunement to the reality around him at all times. His manner of contemplation led to a deeply intentional life; the awareness of God's presence shaped how he lived every moment.

The heartbeat of contemplation for Francis was passionate, consuming desire and willingness to be filled with and led by the Spirit. This desire, present explicitly and implicitly throughout his writings, is summarized in his admonition to his followers to desire "to have the spirit of God at work within them while they pray . . . unceasingly with a heart free from self-interest" ("Rule of 1223," chap. 10). To desire the Spirit is to love God. "Let us love the Lord God with all our heart, all our souls and with all our mind and all our strength and with fortitude and with total understanding, with all of our powers, with every effort, every affection, every emotion, every desire and every wish" ("Rule of 1221," chap. 23).

Some have said that to contemplate is "to look deeply." Francis's heart looked so deeply that he saw God before all else. For him, life itself was in essence contemplative, an ongoing expression of the Holy Spirit. Thomas of Celano reports that Francis considered the Holy Spirit to be the true minister general of the Franciscan order.

Francis showed that contemplation—birthed in the desire for the Holy Spirit, the love for God—means being awake to, attentive to, and in free and deep dialogue with the Spirit within the self, within others, in all living things, in the cosmos, and indeed in all human experience.

We are called to nothing less. If we follow this call, then who we are and how we are on the journey will be shaped by contemplation—contemplation born of awe before the cosmic gift, vigilance to the realities of our world, and gratitude for God's presence in both.

FOLLOWING FRANCIS, FOLLOWING JESUS

Contemplation of the Cosmos

Francis praised the sun for its sovereign gaze over the days of our lives. But he also praised the moon and stars. We cannot see the stars of the universe in the light of the day, when the sun encloses human experience in a dome of our conscious awareness. But gazing upon a night sky, upon the moon and stars, we are more easily led to ask the question: Who are you, God, and who am I?

If the psalmist experienced the night sky as awesome and profoundly humbling, how much more should we do so, given what we now know about our universe? Francis may have looked upon a night sky believing that he was looking up at a celestial dome just above the earth. When we look at the night sky, we know we are not gazing at an enclosed dome but at a universe that contains, by our most recent estimates, upward of 125 billion galaxies. When we look at the Milky Way, we now know that we are staring into the dense center of our galaxy, which astronomers believe is held together by a black hole. Our little solar system, our cosmic address, is located on the outskirts of one of the arms of this galaxy, which contains a few hundred billion stars. It is a member of a small cluster of galaxies (some of which, like Andromeda, can actually be seen by the human eye) traveling together through space as part of a super-cluster of galaxies that contains, scientists estimate, up to a thousand trillion of our suns. These super-clusters of galaxies are separated by vast amounts of empty space that exhaust the mind to contemplate.

It is one thing to feel awe gazing up at the Milky Way, but in recent years our night vision has been wonderfully enhanced by the Hubble Observatory, which can take a photograph of a particular section of deep space that would be the equivalent of the size of a dime at a distance of seventy-five feet. In that photograph Hubble can capture the glimmer of fifteen hundred *galaxies* (not stars).

Having experienced awe at the vastness of the universe, the psalmist asks the question that we too might ask. Given that this planet is an insignificant speck in a small galaxy, how can I attribute any significance to my life? What are human beings that God should be mindful of us? What are mortals that God should care? Here, awe truly begins to take hold of the human spirit. Over against this mind-boggling vastness we still claim by faith that we matter, that every human life has value.

The seemingly infinite vastness of outer space is matched by the infinitesimal nature of subatomic particles. The cosmos is equally awesome in its immensity, its minuteness, and in the "marvelous order [that] predominates in the world of living beings and in the forces of nature" (*Pacem in terris*, no. 2).

Four million years ago we began to walk upright. Through the emergence of consciousness in intelligent life on earth the universe had an opportunity to know itself. Carl Sagan describes humans as "the local embodiment of the Cosmos grown to self-awareness—starstuff pondering the stars; organized assemblages of ten billion, billion, billion atoms considering the evolution of atoms" (Sagan, 345).

Through the scientific and religious consciousness of human beings the universe contemplates itself and beyond itself to our creative source, the God who made heaven and earth. By making us creatures who can see, know, and understand—and are caught up in curiosity, wonder, and awe—we are invited to join the Creator in contemplating and enjoying the masterpiece of creation.

Contemplation and Discipleship

Contemplation is often equated with going to a place alone, apart, quiet, removing oneself from the world, at least for a short time, to focus on God. Francis's life reveals a much broader concept. Although he often sought out places to pray in solitude, he leads us to see contemplation as a constant, a way of living. Conventional wisdom suggests that the contemplative life is the purview only of introverted or introspective people. Those of us who are extroverts or who do not tend toward quiet reflection generally do not see ourselves as likely contemplatives. Francis, by being both extrovert and profoundly contemplative, again gives the lie to conventional wisdom. He invites all to accept the gift of walking a contemplative path.

So we learn from Francis that the contemplative life is not only for people who choose to set themselves apart from the world; nor is it, in the lives of active people, simply reserved for those special moments set apart for attentiveness to God. On the contrary, for Francis, contemplation was how life was led at all moments. We learn from Francis the reality of contemplation as a way of being *in* the world and present to all of creation, not removed from the world.

But where do we find authentic contemplation in action?

It is to be found nowhere else except in the following of Jesus. Within the framework of discipleship we can contemplate history as God's history; we cannot do that anywhere else. Discipleship is the authentic locale of contemplation. It is there that we can see what sin and injustice and what love and hope really are. It is there we can find out who exactly the Son of Man is, the one who preceded us on the same road. Finally, it is there we can find out who exactly is this God who keeps opening out history until he eventually becomes all in all. (Sobrino 1978, 424)

Salvadoran theologian Jon Sobrino recognizes that discipleship and contemplation are integrally connected in the deepest ways; discipleship is the very ground for contemplation. In other words, we cannot truly know Jesus without following Jesus. Only in the following do we undergo the conversion of eyes, ears, and heart that makes it possible for us to see, hear, and respond to the inbreaking of the reign of God all around us.

Contemplation makes it possible for us to see the gospel story being reenacted at the very heart of our own discipleship journey. At the spiritual center of our life we seek to discover in contemplation the gospel story. The dynamic interplay between the gospel story and our own is the subject of contemplation. It is in the contemplative vision that the two stories finally become one.

We know that to be on the discipleship journey means a concrete engagement with history and a struggle against the powers and principalities, those historical forces that thwart and resist the inbreaking reign of God. Sobrino reminds us that only through contemplation expressed in discipleship can we bear to look upon the brutal chaos of history and to see there anything that promises hope and offers redemption. As Sobrino suggests, through contemplation we can see history as God's history—that the reign of God is present even in the negative depths of history. With a contemplative vision the margins of society can be seen not only as places of pain and injustice but of creativity, life, and hope. The contemplative view allows us to behold Christ in the face of the outcast—to recognize that we are accompanied through history by Jesus, who precedes us, opening up history until that moment of final liberation when God becomes "all in all."

Contemplation and Joy

For Francis to be contemplative was a source of great joy. While undoubtedly he had many moments of despondency in his life, he often experienced unbounded joy and ecstasy. To desire God above all else, to hunger and thirst for God, is an expression of the primal need of the human soul—the need for God. In creating us God created within us the hunger for communion with God. To desire God above all else draws us into communion with God and so is the source of deep joy. Perhaps herein lies insight into Francis's joy.

Despite the inevitable difficulties of his vocation as founder of the Franciscan movement, Francis of Assisi must have been a frequent and intimate companion of ecstatic joy. He was a passionate man who blindly and fervently followed his love (Lady Poverty, Christ); desired total union with the suffering and the love of God; saw creatures in their amazing beauty and as manifestations of God; prayed, gazed, and wept for hours in front of the crucifix at San Damiano; ran and leapt barefoot in the fields; was aflame with love, mad with love for God, was a "fool" for God. Bonaventure says, "He was often taken right out of himself in a rapture of contemplation, so that he was lost in ecstasy" (St. Bonaventure, 10:2).

He knew what it was to feel full, overflowing, rich with the intense pleasure of intimate friendship; he experienced the life-giving nature of intimate human relationship in which trust, the sharing of deepest pain and joy, and the bond of the Holy Spirit were assumed.

He drank in the joy of sensuous beauty—the feeling of sunlight on the body, the caress of wind. He must have rejoiced in the exquisite colors that adorned the land of Umbria. He must have seen color as another magnificent manifestation of God's love for creation.

So through Francis we see that to love God intensely and to see God in all human experience—the core of Franciscan contemplation—is a source of profound joy even in the midst of intense suffering and sorrow.

Contemplation: Subversive Presence

What does contemplative joy as Francis knew it offer to contemporary Christians longing and struggling to be people of justice in a society racked with inequity and oppression? The way in which Francis practiced contemplation opened him to an alternative vision of life, life consecrated to the reign of God. Contemplation presents a dramatic challenge to life as we live it—a challenge to consumerism, to power or status-seeking, to inequity, to alienation. (This challenge confronts us both as individuals and as a society.) Imagine for a moment if we were to live a contemplative life—seeing and loving God at the core of all people, seeing that creatures contain God's presence and are in essence a hymn of praise to God, experiencing ecstatic joy, loving passionately. To find boundless joy and passionate love in relationship to God's creation is a radical departure from and contradiction to the norms of a consumer society.

If we as a people allowed ourselves to be filled up with joy and love for the created order, we certainly would not destroy the earth, acquire material affluence at the brutal expense of the world's poor, or wage warfare to protect oil supplies. Could we accept homelessness? Could we fail to protest war? Could we grant the "successful" more respect than the "faltering"?

If we non-poor Christians were both committed to global justice and open to a fraction of the ecstasy, the love, and the Spirit
that Francis experienced, we would be a brilliant and powerful
witness to the New Creation. And we would be sustained for the
path of discipleship.

Contemplation as a way of living calls into question many of
the inequities that we accept in our society. Francis shows us that
the contemplative is moved to be a servant to those in need, to
be in solidarity with the oppressed, to rejoice profoundly, and to
challenge the principalities and powers that create political and
economic inequity. We begin to see that contemplation is the
fertile soil out of which the "fool" of God is begotten.

Contemplation: Doorway to Compassion

In the life of Francis we see that contemplation gives birth to
compassion. Compassion is not to feel *for;* it is to feel *with* and
to be moved to act on behalf of. Compassion, the outstanding
characteristic of Jesus's life, means to have one's guts torn apart
with feeling. Conventional wisdom trains us to be dispassionate
in the face of suffering multitudes, not to see the enormity of
human pain. So shattering and excruciating is the suffering of
so many that we run from it with such practiced dexterity that
we fail even to notice our own running. To face it would be
unbearable; it would paralyze us; it is excruciating. Yet in some
inexplicable way contemplation opens the door to seeing and to
compassion. Is it because contemplation renders our spirit more
deeply connected to living things? Is it seeing Christ in the suffering and Christ accompanying the suffering—the sacrament
of one's neighbor—that enables us, too, to approach, touch, and
suffer deeply with those who suffer? To do so is a tremendous
gift. It makes suffering bearable and helps heal the wounds inflicted by it.

And what of that strange mystery revealed so clearly by Francis: that, for the contemplative, out of the most enormous physical, spiritual, emotional, or existential suffering can be born perfect joy—pure, crystal, divine. In no place is this more evident than in the Canticle of Creation, composed in Francis's most agonizing moments. Reason cannot explain how, in the face of even the most barbaric evil and excruciating suffering, the divine and gracious Presence may be known, especially for the contemplative whose heart finds God in all moments.

Contemplation and the Inner Struggle

Within each of us abides the power for good and for harm, deep-seated passions and energies that may be channeled in life-giving or destructive ways. Contemplation is a source of liberation from the negative, crippling dynamics within us—fears, complexes, addictions, desires, hidden wounds, and a false sense of worthlessness.

In Francis we see one who opened himself to the totality of his psyche. He plumbed his own inner depths, the mystery of his soul, the presence of the life giving and the life destroying within. Facing and struggling with the negative side of his being through contemplation led to profound inner integration and reconciliation that in turn freed him to be reconciled with all of humanity and indeed with all of creation. On one level the Canticle of Creation is a poetic expression of reconciliation and union between Francis and the totality of his being. Although composed by one who had struggled and suffered intensely, it is filled with lightness and devoid of anxiety. This is the song of a soul reconciled with itself and with creation.

Many of us remain enslaved by inner struggles, either by refusing to acknowledge them or by failing to confront and work with them. Francis demonstrates a radically different path, a contemplative approach that trusts in God's loving presence even in the midst of inner gloom. He shows us that when, with true humility, in fear and trembling, and in total reliance upon prayer, we face the negative elements within, we will be met there by an infinitely loving God. If in prayer we aim more to listen to God than to talk to God, then we are blessed by the voice of the One who loves us infinitely and unconditionally. Francis shows us that this encounter with God's love leads both to inner reconciliation and to becoming a reconciling force in the world.

For Francis, fully and humbly facing the struggles within himself was a doorway into a deeper encounter with God. It brought him face to face with the mercy, the boundless love, and the grace of God, which is ever more powerful than sin. Our experience can be the same. As God's beloveds we are the subjects of a love unfathomably magnificent, limitless, and unconditional. Contemplation nourishes a deeper awareness of God's love, which in turn grants us the courage to face the aspects of self from which we run and of which we are afraid. God's accompaniment in that confrontation leads to more profound contemplation.

Contemplation and the Body

There is one gaping hole in Francis's spirituality, a blind spot in his contemplative vision that concerns Francis's spiritual response to the body. Francis, with all his rigor of fasting and poverty, did not always treat his body well; he referred to his body as Brother Ass. Near the end of his life Francis begged forgiveness from Brother Ass, his body, for the sometimes harsh treatment that he inflicted upon it. In a paradox at the heart of his life and witness, Francis was both a sensualist reveling in the pleasures of life and an ascetic rigorously denying the needs of the flesh.

Unfortunately, Francis accepted a dimension of religious practice that scorned and vilified the body until it seemed that to have a body was a reproach and a shame. The original goodness of the body according to the creation stories in Genesis was lost; the body became a vehicle of sin and the primary cause of our fall from grace. Patriarchy and racism used the earthiness of the body as a justification for domination: the more closely identified with the body one was, as women or people of color have been perceived to be, the less one was seen to be made in the image of God.

A genuine biblical spirituality of the body would reclaim our roots in the Hebrew affirmation that the body and soul are an indivisible unity. Such a biblically rooted spirituality is grounded in the reality of the body, its life and death, being young and growing old, waking and sleep, sexual longing and fulfillment, rest and work, sickness and healing. Our bodies are the most visible and immediate sign of our earthiness, our solidarity with the creation. Through our creaturely bodies we are given the gift of our senses. Through our senses we touch, experience, and participate in the goodness of creation and also in its suffering. We celebrate the unity of body and soul when we remember that eating well, resting, and exercising are spiritual disciplines; that addiction to food, drugs, or alcohol is a part of spiritual alienation. The salvation of the soul in some sense involves the healing and wellness of the body.

To lead a fully human life, we must discover harmony between our bodies and our souls. This most certainly means taking simple precautions that ensure the safety of our body, like wearing a seat belt or putting on sun screen. It means getting exercise and observing Sabbath. It means being aware of how we use medications and approach medical care. It means becoming active subjects of our own physical and emotional health, while also being aware of how we affect the well-being of other people's bodies. How do we help our bodies cope with stress? How do we feel about ourselves and express our feelings in general? Our body is a "temple of the Holy Spirit" (1 Cor 6:19), the most fundamental place where we are called to reverence the Creator.

Contemplation and Thanksgiving

Loving God before all else and seeing in all created things a reflection of God—the essence of Franciscan contemplation—called Francis to praise and thank God at every moment in every place, not out of duty or obligation but as a love offering. Francis challenges us to live as though we really believe all that we have and are is a divine gift. If we believed all to be a gift from God, then for the benefit of all we would share with justice, as Francis did, and we would offer our talents primarily in service.

Francis teaches us to look beyond things and circumstances to God, to see the Giver in every gift. "We give you thanks for Yourself." These simple words open chapter 23, entitled "Prayer, Praise, and Thanksgiving," of Francis's "Rule of 1221." These words invite us to praise the Source of All Being regardless of the circumstances in which we find ourselves; even in the most wretched reality, God is present. The prayer, "We give you thanks for Yourself," frees us from the need to possess, to hold onto that which is good, for even when the good is gone, the most important gift remains—the gift of God's self. In his invitation to thanksgiving, Francis once again leads us toward the foolishness of God.

Prayer and Contemplation

Pray all the time, asking for what you need, praying in the Spirit on every possible occasion. (Ephesians 6:18)

The contemplative life as modeled by Jesus and by Francis is in one sense a constant prayer: to be attentive to God in all moments, to see all of creation as sacrament, is to be in prayer. Another way of saying this is that the contemplative life has specific and solid moments before God that we call prayer. Both Jesus and Francis also frequently sought out moments for another form of very personal communion with God. Certainly it would be presumptuous of us to claim much knowledge of these most intimate moments between Francis and God. Yet we can get a glimpse into their nature from the descriptions of Celano and Bonaventure, as well as from the prayers written by Francis.

Francis's times of prayer were very powerful, passionate times in which he received comfort, guidance, and revelations of God's wisdom; conversed intimately with his Love, Christ; interceded on behalf of others; and wrestled with evil. Often he sought out abandoned churches or lonely places in the woods to pray alone. When he returned from prayer he was a man transformed, but he sought never to display the fruits of his communion. Francis's biographers show him praying on every possible occasion, casting all of his cares and needs on God through prayer. "All his attention and affection he directed with his whole being to the one thing which he was asking of the Lord, not so much praying as becoming himself a prayer" (Celano, *Second Life,* no. 95). Prayer helped him to remain attentive to God's presence, to live in contemplation. Francis derived profound pleasure from prayer, his soul in prayer receiving its food, which was God.

Perhaps it is true that for many contemporary Christians, in contrast, not having experienced prayer as life-giving contact with God, it is hard to find reason to pray. Countless people of faith have intense and fruitful lives of frequent prayer, but for others, prayer can tend to be pushed to the wayside or relegated to mealtime, bedtime, and Sunday morning rituals. To be sure, even good-willed people of faith are only aware of the form of prayer in which they briefly address God, either alone or in groups, with words, usually of praise or petition. The deeper prayer of Francis, which includes stillness before God, listening to God, and communing fervently with God, is largely unfamiliar to them.

Today's world presents many powerful barriers to the way of prayer of Christians. One is the tendency to think we don't need it. We get along fine without prayer. We have technology, wealth, and power to supply our needs. Prayer seems superfluous, almost superstitious. Another barrier is that we are accustomed to getting results. We expect results, and when we pray we often don't seem to get them. With prayer, it may seem that God does not respond, or that God responds in a way that we do not like, or that we just do not know whether or not God responds. This question of response especially impedes prayers of petition and thanksgiving. We may not want to thank God when "good" things happen because so doing might imply that God is either heartless or powerless in the face of the "bad" things.

Perhaps the biggest barrier to prayer is that we don't trust it. We know that prayer won't protect us from excruciating pain; we know that Christians who pray experience torture, agonizing death, and unbearable losses. And finally, at times we simply may feel too exhausted by daily life or too full of despair in the face of human suffering to pray. So why pray?

What response does Francis's life offer to our unspoken, Why pray? Francis's guide was the example of Jesus, who invites us by his example and summons us by his words to dialogue with God. The Gospels portray Jesus as one who prayed deeply. Like Moses, Elijah, the Galilean holy men of his time, and others to the tradition in which Jesus stood, he frequently withdrew in solitude for prayer. "In the morning a great while before day, he rose and went out to a lonely place and there he prayed" (Mark 1:35). Jesus in word and deed shows that prayer is essential to the discipleship journey. For us, as for Francis, following Jesus leads to prayer.

Finally, to pray as an element of following Jesus is an act of freedom. It is a stance of freedom from all of the societal forces that lead many sincere Christians to give up prayer. (Bonaventure describes Francis wrestling intensely with the temptation not to pray.) It is freedom from dependence upon one's own motivation to pray. It doesn't matter if we are discouraged, despairing, or exhausted. Jesus invites us to pray; he offers to feed us with prayer. Francis knew that freedom. He prayed in all circumstances—in suffering, in joy, when facing danger, or in seeing beauty. Prayer offers the freedom to believe in the face of disbelief. Even when we feel abandoned, or overwhelmed, or believe that our prayer disappears into emptiness, Jesus shows us that the relationship with God is present even in God's apparent absence. "My God, my God, why hast thou forsaken me?" (Matt 27:46). Francis joyfully accepted the freedom offered by the discipline of prayer.

Prayer was, for Francis, essential sustenance. So can it be for us. How can we possibly hear and respond to the other calls of Christ without the sustenance of prayer? Without prayer can we confront violence, the powers that separate us into rich and poor, the forces that destroy the earth, despair and pain, and the temptation to sleep while Jesus (and our neighbor) is in agony? Indeed, for many who have sought to face evil in its awesome dimensions, we pray because we know that in the end evil cannot be overcome without prayer. To pray in the face of evil is to proclaim the New Creation in the moment at hand.

As Francis so clearly experienced, prayer engenders intimacy between the human person and God. Prayer nurtures the faith that God knows one intimately and that the initiative for relationship with God lies with God; it is a gift. In praying we trust that "before they call I will answer; while they are yet speaking I will hear" (Isa 65:24). We are assured that even when we do not know what to pray, "the Spirit expresses our plea with sighs too deep for words" (Rom 8:26). When we continue to pray until we hear God, rather than concentrating solely on being heard by God, then prayer reveals to us, as it did to Francis, the infused love of God within us and within all creation. To pray like Francis requires a leap of faith.

By Grace Alone

Franciscan contemplation certainly poses a challenge to the spiritual life of contemporary Christians. Many things take precedence over God in determining our decisions, priorities, and lifestyles. It seems almost impossible to love God before all else, to see the Spirit first in all experience. We may find ourselves backing away from Francis, seeing contemplative living as something that Francis achieved but too far from our reality even to consider. Yet to do so would be a terrible mistake. Francis did not rise to this state of being. Rather, it was a free gift from God, which he accepted. Francis reveals that to know the Spirit and to follow Jesus are divine gifts ultimately dependent upon God's grace. In Francis's words, "By Your grace alone, may we make our way to You."

Grace—the ceaseless and immeasurable outpouring of God's love for us that offers healing, reconciliation, and illumination—is not at all contingent upon our worthiness. Grace is a mystery that the human cannot fathom and even in art, music, or poetry can only begin to describe as did Francis in the Canticle of Creation. We must be willing to participate in this mystery, not by comprehension but by faith.

The gifts of loving God and following Christ are given not only to Francis but also to us; we need only accept them. Francis must have understood the amazing truth that God loves us and claims us out of God's pure goodness, not because of any merit on our part; that in response to God's love we are called to love and serve God and God's creation; and, furthermore, that God's love for us is far greater and more magnificent than we can imagine. Francis—God's fool—was one who knew profoundly God's grace and responded to it. This divine foolishness is offered to us all.

Trusting in this grace, clinging to the promise that nothing can separate us from God, accepting the free gift of loving presence presents us with a paradox: We can do nothing to earn this gift, yet the paths we choose may serve either to blind us to God's grace or open us up to know it, to accept it gratefully, and to respond. We may be blinded by hearts, minds, and attention so cluttered with fears, activities, and desires that we have no space to receive grace. What, then, are the paths that open us to grace?

First, Francis's conversion process shows us that by seeking to follow Jesus rather than false gods we become more aware of God's love. Precisely because grace is inseparable from following Jesus, ultimately it is, using Bonhoeffer's word, costly.

Second, Francis shows us that grace is revealed profoundly in the deserts of our lives. Whatever our private or public deserts may be—agonizing pain, battles with attachments, repentance and conversion, confrontation with evil—the living water of God's grace transforms the desert to a garden and brings conversion and a deepened knowledge of God's mysterious love. In the desert lands where the Jewish, Christian, and Muslim traditions were born, living water became and has remained a powerful symbol of God's grace.

We cannot help but remember the desert that Francis experienced after he had received the stigmata. Bleeding, blind, exhausted by forty days of fasting, and his eyes in searing pain, he lay for forty more days in a house adjacent to the monastery of San Damiano. His soul, too, was in agony as he witnessed Christendom, and indeed some within the brotherhood, shunning the values of peace, simplicity, and poverty that he considered essential to discipleship. Celano suggests that conflict raged in Francis's soul and that he prayed not to be overcome by discouragement. It was in this desert that God spoke to him. Francis heard, was filled with utter joy, and composed the Canticle of Creation, that magnificent testimony to grace.

So Francis lights our path with a model of contemplative discipleship born in a trust that the embrace of God's love is ever with us, is abundant beyond our imagining, and is neither initiated by us nor dependent upon us. Understanding that contemplation was given to Francis, not attained by him, and trusting that we are no less beloved of God than was Francis, we too can accept the grace-filled invitation to contemplative discipleship, taste the sweetness of the Spirit in every reality, respond with deeper love, and dare to follow the costly path of Jesus. Indeed we, too, will be fools for God.

At the core of Franciscan spirituality is contemplation. To be contemplative is to love above all else the one true God. Out of that love is born the "fool" of God. Jesus was the ultimate fool of God. Francis, following Jesus, was the fool. Contemplation leads the fool to see God in the leper, to walk unarmed into the enemy camp, to talk with creatures as brother and sister, to relinquish wealth and privilege, to rebuild the church. This is certainly not, according to the world, a pragmatic path, but one can hardly be pragmatic with a leader like Jesus.

OUR STORIES

Allow each of your senses to find a voice—to tell the story of its interaction with God and with creation. To do this you might employ the *examen,* a technique common in Ignatian prayer of reflection on the events of the day in order to detect God's presence and discern God's call in our lives. At the end of a day ask yourself: What did I see today, really see? What did I hear? Did I taste the food I ate? Who and what did I touch? What do my senses teach me about myself, about God, about creation?

Create a timeline of your life from the perspective of your body. Tell the story of your body through the process of being born; growing up as child; expanding into the fullness of your adult life; discovering your sexuality; your memories of sickness and health, of the brokenness of body and its healing; experience of aging and moments of mortality.

SIGNS OF OUR TIMES

St. Augustine once said that God continually tries to give us good things, but our hands are too full to receive them. God offers us the kind of relationship with God and with creation that grows in a contemplative life. Yet for most of us our hands are too full to receive this offer. Many features of life in contemporary society draw us away from a contemplative way of living. Our time, energy, and attention go in many directions. Consequently, we do not focus on the Spirit within each moment. We resist the contemplative. We fail to stand in awe before the spectacular beauty, order, and purposefulness in the story of the universe. We fail to mourn the loss of a life, the abuse of a child, the brutality of war, the destruction of a species, the disruption of earth's climate.

Many aspects of our lives draw us away from contemplative living: a frenzied pace of life; the need for excitement and stimulation; the need to achieve; family and friends; political work; jobs; the desire for more money or nicer things; and on and on. Many are important and life giving; others are destructive at worst and superfluous at best.

The denial of the goodness of the body that has plagued the Christian tradition also has been an obstacle to our contemplative relationship with the Creator present in all creation and a mirror image of the contemporary cult of the perfect body. This cult of the perfect body, so prevalent in our society, also denies the goodness of our bodies and gives a false definition of beauty and human identity.

According to Paul Hawken, molecular biologist Mahlon Hoagland

> *estimates it would require 1,500 encyclopedias to create an owner's manual for one person. The exquisite integration of movement, thought, physiology, sight, touch, and*

> *metabolism supersedes the complexity of any other system we can imagine. Something operates us, but what? Is it not the free flow of brilliant and ancient information, an involuntary intelligence freely exchanged on the cellular and intracellular level? (Hawken, 177)*

The body's wisdom is the beautiful artistry of our loving Creator.

INVITATION TO RESPOND

All questions of identity for the Christian lead us back to the foundation of Christian spirituality, the imago Dei, the affirmation that we are made in the image of God. This is the divine wellspring of goodness that flows from deep within us, washing over the totality of who we are: our psyche, our emotions, our body. How did the Christian tradition stray so far from this affirmation of the goodness of the body? And how do we begin to reclaim the role of the body in our spiritual lives, our contemplative relationship with the Creator present in all creation? How do we as spiritual beings begin to reinhabit our bodies? Perhaps we begin by listening to them.

• Imagine a conversation between yourself and your body. Imagine your body as a "thou" rather than an "it," a "thou" that can speak to you and has very important things to say. Consider your body to be your trusted spiritual director. What would your body as spiritual director have to say to you in your development as a human being, in your faith pilgrimage? Is it the rediscovery of your sexuality? Is it the cost of dealing with the stress of life? Is it aging? Is it body image? Could it be your response to longstanding health issues? In this dialogue with your body, what would you say? Do we disregard what our body says to us? Where do we fall in that spectrum of attitude toward the body?

What do you think about your body? In what ways do you honor and nurture your body, and in what ways do you not? Are we practicing faithful stewardship of that part of creation with which we have been most intimately entrusted? What are the barriers that keep you from a full affirmation of your body? Take some time to affirm the goodness of your body in its capacity for work and play, for solitude and communion, for healing and wholeness, for love and prayer.

• Turn to the Appendix, "A Reflection on the Canticle of Creation." The canticle embraces a cosmic meaning; Francis is celebrating the gifts of God's creation. Each of the praises and all of them together also have profoundly spiritual meaning. Eloi Leclerc, OFM, has opened up new understandings of the canticle as a synthesis of personal spirituality and cosmic mysticism. Take time with the meditations on each stanza of the canticle. With each of the cosmic elements found in the Canticle of Creation, we can look within to an inward ecology. Francis's canticle teaches us that when we open our hearts in gratitude to the Creator for the beauty and wonder of creation, we simultaneously lay hold of deeply spiritual truths at the core of our being.

9

Francis and Creation

Dialogue with the Source of All Being

For the creation waits with eager longing for the reveal-ing of the children of God; We know that all creation is groaning in labor pains even until now; and not only that, but we ourselves, who have the first fruits of the Spirit, we also groan within ourselves as we wait for adoption, the redemption of our bodies. For in hope we were saved. (Romans 8:19, 22–24)

The heavens declare the glory of God, and the firmament proclaims his handiwork. Day pours out the word to day, and night to night imparts knowledge; Not a word nor a discourse whose voice is not heard; Through all the earth their voice resounds, and to the ends of the world, their message. (Psalm 19:1–5)

FRANCIS'S STORY

Francis of Assisi

The countryside around Assisi in which Francis grew up was very important to him. He had a great love for the farmlands around the city and for the wilderness of mountain, river, and forest. This love for the natural world shaped the identity of Francis, the expression of his spirituality and mission. Many stories describe Francis and his encounters with the natural world—with animals, birds, fish, and even insects. He walked reverently on stones; he rejoiced in the sound of running water or blowing wind. Francis had a special love for living creatures; they seemed to sense in him a gentle, loving presence. Above all, as Francis turned to God and was gripped by the reality of the Incarnation, nature became holy for him. Everything created by God had also been touched by the presence of the Word made flesh. Francis was not only a lover of nature and a poet who saw great beauty in all that was around him, he also was deeply enthralled by God's presence in the created order.

During the time when (as has been said) many joined themselves to the brethren the most blessed father Francis was journeying through the valley of Spoleto, and came to a spot near Bevagna where a very great number of birds of different sorts were gathered together, viz. doves, rooks, and those other birds that are called in the vulgar tongue monade. When he saw them, being a man of the most fervent temper and also very tender and affectionate toward all the lower and irrational creatures, Francis the most blessed servant of God left his companions in the way and ran eagerly toward the birds.

When he was come close to them and saw that they were awaiting him, he gave them his accustomed greeting. But, not a little surprised that the birds did not fly away (as they are wont to do) he was filled with exceeding joy and humbly begged them to hear the word of God: and, after saying many things to them he added, "My brother birds, much ought you to praise your Creator, and ever to love Him who has given you feathers for clothing, wings for flight and all that you had need of. God has made you noble among His creatures, for He has given you a habitation in the purity of the air, and, whereas you neither sow nor reap, He himself does still protect and govern you without any care of your own." On this (as he himself and the brethren who had been with him used to say) those little birds, rejoicing in wondrous fashion, after their nature, began to stretch out their necks, to spread their wings, to open their beaks and to gaze on him. And then he went to and fro amidst them, touching their heads and bodies with his tunic. At length he blessed them, and, having made the sign of the Cross, gave them leave to fly away to another place. (Celano, First Life, no. 58)

In every work of the artist he praised the Artist; whatever he found in the things made he referred to the Maker. He rejoiced in all the works of the hands of the Lord and saw behind things pleasant to behold their life-giving reason and cause. In beautiful things he saw Beauty itself; all things were to him good. "He who made us is the best," they cried out to him. Through his footprints impressed upon things he followed the Beloved everywhere, he made for himself from all things a ladder by which to come even to his throne. . . . For that original goodness that will be one day all things in all already shown forth in this saint all things in all. (Celano, Second Life, no. 165)

In contrast to Francis's understanding of the divine presence in creation, we have become a people who, having lost the sense of the divine presence, are intent on destroying nature.

The painful wounds inflicted on creation by human hands have led to a deepening ecological crisis on a planetary scale that we now know will lead to catastrophe. Twenty years ago, when *St. Francis and the Foolishness of God* was first published, human civilization across this planet was at a crossroads; severe climate change might yet be averted if major changes were initiated immediately. That can no longer be said; we are no longer at a crossroads. By the collective action and inaction of our civilization, we are well down the path toward planetary crisis. Finding ourselves in this profound ecological crisis forces the faith community to be critical of our theological tradition and practice. How has the worldview of the church contributed to the deepening crisis in the ecosystem? The current ecological crisis is a theological crisis for us; as the church, we must wrestle with the painful reality that our theology, worship, and ministry not only have failed to defend creation but also have contributed to its exploitation and destruction.

To open this reflection we need to let go of sentimental notions of a Francis associated with birdbaths and assorted backyard statuary and claim a relationship with him as a guide, as a spiritual companion, and as the patron saint of the environment.

The Good News of the Incarnation: Word Made Flesh

The story of how Francis began the tradition of the living Christmas nativity is an interesting place to begin. St. Francis was drawn to the birth of Christ for its simplicity, humility, and poverty, and he greatly desired to kindle within his brothers and among the people of Assisi a similar devotion to the drama of Christmas. So he created a living nativity scene near a cave in the woods outside of Assisi with a manger and all the animals that one might expect on a farm. Francis celebrated the good news of Christ's birth that embraces all living creatures, indeed all of creation, understanding that the Incarnation, the Word made flesh, was the foundation for a spiritual affirmation of the goodness of creation. The manger is a sign that the animal world, indeed all of nature, participates in welcoming the Christ child who brings peace to all the earth. In the birth of the Christ child, God has enacted cosmic peace. Such a peace is not just among people but between people and the rest of the earth community as well.

The Sacred Book: The Word of God Spoken in Scripture and in Creation

The creation story that begins Genesis makes the foundational affirmation that all of creation is a word of God. The mystic Meister Eckhart once wrote:

> *Apprehend God in all things for God is in all things. Every single creature is full of God and is a book about God. Every creature is a word of God. If I spent enough time with the tiniest creature—even a caterpillar—I would never have to prepare a sermon; so full of God is every creature. (Brussat, 167)*

And Wendell Berry writes: "Outdoors we are confronted everywhere with wonders; we see that the miraculous is not extraordinary but the common mode of existence. It is our daily bread" (Berry, 103). Most important, Jesus, the Word made flesh, often pointed to the sacred book of nature: "Consider the birds of the air . . . and the lilies of the field" (Matt 6:26–28).

Stephen Mitchell, a Buddhist scholar who has brought new insight into the interpretation of Christian scriptures, writes that when Jesus said to consider the lilies of the field and the birds of the air, he was inviting people into a state of being, a way of being at ease among the joys and sorrows of our world. It is possible, Jesus teaches us, to be as simple and beautiful as the birds of the sky and the lilies of the field, which are always within the eternal now.

Nowhere is this intimate relationship between the two sacred books of scripture and nature expressed more eloquently than in Psalm 19. One half of the psalm celebrates the gift of Torah, the sacred book of scripture given to Israel. The other half celebrates the sacred book of creation: "Day to day pours forth speech and night to night declares knowledge. There is no speech, their voice is not heard, yet their voice goes out to all the earth and their words to the end of the world" (Ps 19:2–4). C. S. Lewis considered Psalm 19 to be the greatest poem in the Bible and one of the greatest lyrics in the history of the world.

Normally a psalm begins with a summons to the faithful to raise a song of praise to God, but in Psalm 19 this invitation is omitted because the hymn of praise has already begun. Eons ago at the time of creation the notes were first sounded. The heavens proclaimed God's handiwork. The created universe around us reveals the skillful design and loving intention of a master artist, our Creator.

But creation's witness to the artistry of the Creator did not end with a primordial moment of creation. There is neither pause nor break but a continuous testimony of rapturous joy. "Day to day pours forth speech and night to night declares knowledge"—the supreme expression of Hebrew poetry found in the psalms. Nature has unceasingly proclaimed God's glory since the beginning of creation. Every day of the week, every week of the year, year after year, eon after eon, the created order testifies to the Creator in unfailing, continuous praise.

This testimony of praise found in the psalms is exuberant and effusive, responding to the reality of life in a reliable, generous, gift-giving world. The language is doxological and lyrical. It is, as Walter Brueggemann testifies, language that soars, cut free to match the extravagance of God. Just as Israel participates in covenant with the Creator, so does all creation. This covenant, in its essence, is the ongoing interaction of gift and gratitude. Psalm 19 calls us to imagine that all of nature enjoys a relationship to God. In some mysterious sense nature knows God and is able to praise God and bear witness to the life-giving abundance of divine Love.

St. Francis, who called all creatures brother and sister, understood this when he preached to the birds and exhorted them to sing praise. All creatures are our brothers and sisters in the family of God. God is teaching all creatures to praise God in their own language for the beauty and wonder of creation and to give thanks for the abundant gifts of life.

God in All Things

The creation spirituality of St. Francis is not *pantheism*—the idea that God and nature are the same. Creation spirituality from a Franciscan or Christian perspective is *pan-entheism*, God in creation; God in everything; everything in God. Creation spirituality is a posture that seeks to behold and respond to the mystery of the divine being that shimmers in all creatures, great and small. Through the Canticle of Creation, Francis expressed a sense of mystical union with all that is, calling out to all of creation as brother and sister. This is the spiritual center of the Franciscan worldview. Everything created—the earth, the oceans, plants and animals, rocks and waters, everything animate and inanimate—deserves brotherly love and sisterly respect. On the basis of this mysticism of universal brotherhood and sisterhood—the kinship of all life—Francis treated all things with respect and tenderness. He told his associates not to cut the trees down completely so that they could grow again, and not to take all the bees' honey, lest they starve. Legends abound about Francis preaching to the birds. Creatures seemed to respond to him without fear. Birds would gather around him and chirp as he called them to rejoice with him in the glory of the Creator. His love and respect for all his brothers and sisters in creation was the driving force behind Francis's ecological vision.

The Canticle of Creation

A uniquely Franciscan vision of such a transformed relationships with creation is found in the Canticle of Creation. God is the source of all being. Creator God is the Parent, both Mother and Father of all creatures, who are therefore brother and sister to one another. Because all of creation is a part of this divine family, everything created, animate and inanimate, deserves brotherly and sisterly love and respect. The divine image or spark, the imago Dei that exists in humans, exists in all creatures. This divine image exists even in the "cornfields and vineyards . . . stones and forests . . . beautiful things of the field . . . fountains of water." In each stanza of the canticle, Francis invokes a cosmic element that in its own right is praising the Creator. The voice of humankind praising the Creator is not a solo voice but part of a chorus, a cosmic choir made up of all God's creatures. The sun, the moon, and the earth praise the Creator.

FOLLOWING FRANCIS, FOLLOWING JESUS

Francis is a model for a transformed human life because of the unique way that he followed Christ, the New Adam in a redeemed paradise. The late Rev. Bennett Sims, Episcopal bishop and author, in his book *Servanthood: Leadership for the Third Millennium*, makes the case that Jesus is the prototype of an entirely new level of evolving humanity, the first-born *hetero pacificus* (peaceable humanity), who will bring a new species of creature into being. Theologically speaking, Jesus is the New Adam who opens a way for us to become the full and complete humanity intended by the Creator, capable of awe, ecstasy, gratitude, and praise for the gift of creation, and for whom "all creation waits with eager longing."

Walking Humbly with God and Creation

Francis reveled in the glory of God in creation. He lived out of a sense of ecstatic union with God's presence in all things. Francis called out to all the world in warm greetings: Brother! Sister! The nature of this encounter could be described in the language of the Jewish theologian Martin Buber as an "I-Thou" encounter. Buber recognized that reality is fundamentally two kinds of relationships. The impersonal, subject-object, "I-It" relationship is extended to all so-called objects, and in actuality to most human beings; the "I-Thou" relationship is experienced in moments that honor the sacredness of human identity and personal relationship. Francis extends this "I-Thou" relationship to everything. He invites us to see with him that the true nature of reality is expressed in the "I-Thou" relationship between God the Creator and all of creation. God is the God of sky, land, water, and all life. Everything has a relationship with God. Seeing this, we are invited to greet with gratitude all things as exuding the goodness of God.

Francis's Canticle of Creation is not just nice poetry. It is a profound celebration of creation. The canticle names reality as constituted in the relationship of all things as brother and sister, inviting humans to understand our destiny in the created world as a very simple one, that of walking in paradise. Francis lived out of an essential vision of paradise, a vision of God's original design for creation that will be again when Creator and creation are reconciled, when God becomes "all in all." As the New Creation comes into being, we must be as present as possible to its unfolding: look for its signs and wonders, and hear its groaning. Francis did this. It set him apart from others; within the world that is, he could see the wonder of the world to be. This is what Celano meant when he said that Francis had "already escaped into the freedom of the glory of the children of God" (*First Life*, no. 81). Francis experienced in an anticipatory way the future to which we are all called. He was present to this New Creation because of his own transformation. The spirit of the canticle has the power to enkindle within us a new longing for paradise as the harmonious communion of all creatures.

In Francis of Assisi we have a companion and guide who teaches us to walk on the face of the earth with humility and with an open and grateful heart, aware of the divine goodness in all things. To do this, we must first let go of a self-understanding that is profoundly grandiose. To know our place on the earth is to respect boundaries and limits. When we think of ourselves as over and above creation, when we think of the world as a collection of "its" put there for us to exploit, we are participating in a worldview that allows, rationalizes, even encourages the exploitation of nature. To recover an ecological humility, we both affirm our worth as individuals and as a species that is part of the earth community and, at the same time, acknowledge our relative insignificance in the face of the spectacular scientific discoveries about the size and complexity of the cosmos. This new humility is historically analogous to the moment when Copernicus said to church and European society that the earth is not the center of the universe.

We are being called to accept a place in creation that, however special, is not central. We humans must dethrone ourselves as tyrannical rulers of the universe. Only with this humility, this proper sense of self, can we recognize the intricate web of life on which we, with all other creatures, depend. Then we are able to begin to address every other creature as sister and brother, deserving of respect, compassion, and reverence. The witness of Francis calls us to repent of the pride that leads to domination and alienation. With Franciscan humility we can move in repentance from greed to thanksgiving and from exploitation to trust. We can recover a sense of the sacredness of life and place and matter. As we give thanks for all good things coming from the hand of

God, we recognize the intrinsic relationality of all creation, from the microscopic to the cosmic.

With Francis we realize that the gift of creation is also a call to responsibility. Created in the image of God, humanity's vocation is to participate fully with God in creating a world of peace, social justice, and right relationships with creation. Much debate will continue in theological and ecological circles regarding humankind's role in relation to creation. For some, to speak of a human calling to stewardship of creation is highly problematic, implying that we humans are granted special freedoms and responsibilities to control and manipulate creation. For others, stewardship conveys the sense that we are entrusted to be "gardeners" within the earth's garden—that we are called not to manipulate but to nourish and protect creation.

Human beings possess the capacity for self-conscious reflection and moral awareness; we can know the impact of our choices and we can change them. We must use this gift of consciousness well, examining critically the theological imagery that we use to describe our relationship to the created order. This is an important and unfinished dialogue that is central to our mission to care for the earth and to do eco-justice. How we understand the divine image within is likely to determine how we do this work.

The journey out of the environmental crisis will be dangerous and consuming. Francis gives us three gifts for the journey: vision, faith, and vocation:

• a vision of creation as paradise in which every creature is sister and brother to us, a "thou" deserving love and respect; faith that God is within us and within the rest of creation—that to recognize the divine image in humanity is to accept humbly our place in the created order that sustains all life; and

• a vocation grounded in the hope for a New Creation that God is bringing about in the celebration of life and in the struggle for justice on earth.

Our Stories

In the exercises that follow, reflect on your encounters with creation at different points in your life.

• What was the geography of your childhood? Did you grow up in an urban, suburban, or rural setting? Did you play outdoors? Did you have any pets? Did you ever raise plants or crops? What are positive and negative memories of your childhood experiences of nature? How do you think those circumstances shaped your view of nature? How have those childhood experiences of nature shaped your identity as an adult?

• Have you ever experienced moments of communion with nature, times when the distance between you and the rest of creation was bridged or overcome? Where and how did this happen? What did you feel? Did these experiences change the way you view the world?

• Have you ever been confronted with the wounds inflicted on the natural world by humankind? Describe this encounter. What feelings did you have? Who or what was responsible for this wounding of the environment? What was your response?

Signs of Our Times

Return to Romans 8: "We know that the whole creation has been groaning in travail together until now, and not only the creation but we ourselves who have the first fruits of the Spirit, groan inwardly as we await our adoption as sons and daughters and the redemption of our bodies."

What sense can we make today of Paul's idea of the groaning of creation? Can we as people of faith learn to hear the groans of creation? Listen! Can we hear the groaning of creation in the sound of a giant Arctic ice shelf crashing into the water? Can we hear the muted cries and whispers of a river that is being drained dry? Listen! Can we hear the groaning of rainforests being cut down, of skies polluted, of dead zones in our oceans? Can we hear the sound of entire species disappearing every day? This is the groaning of creation.

There is groaning too among God's people. Our bodies are a sign of our solidarity with the whole of creation. We are not separate, not above; we are a part of this earth. The sickness we inflict upon the earth we inflict upon ourselves. As creation groans, so do we. But Paul goes further, suggesting that not only is creation groaning, and human beings, but God as well; the Holy Spirit groans with and through creation.

Paul offers a prophetic challenge to the church of today to listen to the groaning of the created order in the many environmental challenges that we face, but he also calls us to an audacious hopefulness. With Paul, we are called to understand the groaning of earth as the birth pangs of a New Creation. God, our loving and faithful Creator, hears the cries of the earth and is moving to protect and restore it. God loves, bringing forth a New Creation. This is the horizon of hope to which the gospel calls us: a transformed earth, a New Creation.

Reading the Canticle as a Lens into the Global Ecological Crisis

As we move to restore the earth, we are called to see creation as the *anawim*, the biblical word for the ones whose voices are not heard. We are to be advocates for a wounded creation. We are called to accompany creation precisely at the point of its wounds, those places of brokenness and despoliation. The crucified God in solidarity with the brokenness of creation is also the God of resurrection, able to bring healing out of sickness, reconciliation out of alienation, and life out of death. To be faithful to the crucified and risen One present in creation, we must participate in this divine work of healing and reconciling creation. We are faced with what is undoubtedly the most monumental challenge ever faced by humankind. With all people of good will we are increasingly clear that our challenge is to live within the boundaries of our garden paradise.

People in the global North face this challenge recognizing that we have used an inordinate percentage of the planet's resources and are largely responsible for the climate crisis. Having reaped the benefits of a growth-focused and consumption-driven global economy, we now owe a tremendous ecological debt to people in the global South.

Let us join Francis in singing and living the Canticle of Creation.

All Praise Be Yours for Brother Sun

Today human society is bringing new attention to the reality of the sun. We understand that life exists on this planet at all because of the perfect proximity to our sun. Earth is a "Goldilocks" planet, not too hot and not too cold but "just right." Any farther away from our star, and this planet would be frozen. Any closer and it would be burned up. (Astronomers now estimate that there may be literally billions of Goldilocks planets in our galaxy alone.) The philosopher Buckminster Fuller writes that we are all passengers on Spaceship Earth, which is powered by a mother ship, the sun. To sustain Spaceship Earth for future generations we need to meet our energy needs with renewable resources, especially solar energy. Dipping into the carbon bank of the past for oil or coal overwhelms the waste absorption capacity of earth. Moving away from a global economy that is dependent on fossil fuels is a huge challenge. May the sun help us to imagine a transformed energy future and call us to undertake the great shift of our civilization from fossil fuels to sustainable energy.

All Praise Be Yours for Sister Earth

With Francis, Christianity can learn to look upon the earth as "thou"! The environmental writer Paul Hawken in his book *Blessed Unrest* (Hawken, 141) says that earth is not a machine that we operate and use for whatever technological purpose within our power. Earth is one living organism characterized by complex, life-giving interdependence. Earth is a living organism with a skeleton of ancient geological formations; a circulation system of oceans, seas, rivers, and creeks; a respiratory system of rainforests by which the earth breathes. Earth is one body doing everything that our bodies do—constantly renewing itself, recycling waste, cleansing, healing itself.

Most inspiring is Hawken's image that the global environmental movement is functioning like the immune system of an organism that fights off illness and disease. Across this planet thousands upon thousands of individuals and communities are attacking toxins, cleaning up waste and pollution, undoing our dependence on fossil fuels, seeking to restore nature's harmony and balance. People of faith and good will are working with earth to bring about global healing. We don't manage the immune system of earth any more than we manage the immune system of our bodies, but we protect our bodies, nurture our bodies, listen to them, and tend to them with food, sleep, prayer, friendship, laughter, and exercise—and that is all the planet asks of us. The planet needs human beings to be allies who will respect and nurture the earth, who will engage with the earth in a holy collaboration of healing.

All Praise Be Yours for Sister Water

There is a growing awareness that the nations and peoples of the world are competing for the increasingly scarce resource, water. Access to clean water and who owns and controls it is becoming a defining political reality of our world. In that sobering context there are signs of hope around the world, specifically in South Africa whose progressive water policies are now being studied around the world. Over the last twenty years water managers, legislators, activists, and others have worked together to bring about a shift in how water is seen and managed. The twentieth century viewed water as an economic asset, the sole purpose of which was to be converted into energy, irrigate fields, or supply cities.

In South Africa, however, there is a growing understanding that if rivers are to continue to supply humans with what they need to survive, water itself has to flourish. Nature is like a blood donor; if the donor doesn't have enough blood in her body, she will die, and all who need her blood will die with her. It is inconceivable to drain the donor dry. South Africa is considered a world leader in water conservation because there, only nature and people have an absolute right to water. All other users are secondary. This shift would turn water laws and policies on their head in much of the world.

Consider the Colorado River in North America. It is a lifeline sustaining the western states of Wyoming, California, Utah, Colorado, Arizona, Nevada, and New Mexico. Because of plunging volume, the waters of the Colorado no longer reach their destination at the Sea of Cortez in Mexico, thus depriving the Mexican people of their birthright to the river. Drought intensified by climate change and the increasing population of the West are draining the life out of the Colorado. All seven western states that share the waters of the Colorado River are on a collision course between supply and demand. The only answer is to recognize that western US water policy is hopelessly unsustainable. All the southwestern states must reduce their water consumption and embrace an ethic of sustainable water use.

All Praise Be Yours for Those Who Grant Pardon for Love of You, Through Those Who Endure Sickness and Trial

The destruction of global habitat has had a devastating impact on biodiversity and on indigenous peoples everywhere. Indigenous communities have suffered tremendously, but there is something in their relatedness to the earth that has allowed them to continue to affirm life and to continue the struggle in hope. All over the world indigenous communities are resisting the on-going conquest of the earth. The Dayak peoples of Borneo face the destruction of their homelands from extensive clearcutting of primary forests and from water pollution from oil companies. The Ogoni people of Nigeria have seen the rich Niger River delta devastated by oil pollution and toxic wastes. The Kogi tribe in Colombia faces extermination due to US aerial spraying of herbicides designed to prevent the cultivation of coca. The Garifuna of Honduras are protesting the construction of resorts on expropriated lands. The San people of Botswana have been banished from ancestral lands in favor of tourism and diamond mining. The Aboriginal peoples of Australia confront radiation spills from uranium mining. In Chile and Argentina the indigenous peoples are standing up to mining interests pursuing an open-pit gold-mining operation that will destroy three different glaciers (Hawken, 104).

Tragically, this litany of conquest goes on and on. But in inspiring ways, so does the story of heroic resistance by indigenous peoples struggling to preserve the earth and themselves. Indigenous communities are leading the way with a vision of the sacredness of life and the natural world. They are leading in the reform of global policies to ensure not only the rights of all human beings present and future to have access to the blessings of nature but the right of nature itself.

There is an inescapable element of environmental racism in the reality of climate change. People of color currently bear the brunt of the global consequences of the collective sin of the industrialized nations. This disparity will continue and deepen unless we recognize and change it. Privileged citizens of the global North must be in dialogue with the marginalized to hear clearly the cries of creation, for they are the ones who experience most directly creation's wounds. This is equally true in communities across the United States. The environmental problems that afflict our society as a whole are on the doorstep of communities of color. Three out of five Hispanic and African Americans live in communities with uncontrolled toxic-waste dumps. The race and economic status of nearby residents are the leading factors in the location of commercial and hazardous waste facilities. Impoverished and marginalized people alone can teach our church and society about the critical link between justice and the environment.

INVITATION TO RESPOND

Every global issue is first a local issue. It may be difficult at times to see how our actions can have an impact at the global level. It is easier to know what to do about our own neighborhood than about rain forests in the Amazon. But somehow we must continue to hold these struggles together. Global change is most likely to happen when each of us stands firmly rooted and remembers our interconnectedness.

The Global: An Economy of Right Relationships

Around the world life's basic resources are becoming more scarce. Food insecurity, rising sea levels, warming temperatures, the frequency of terrifying storms, and the accelerated extinction of species already are having dire consequences for humans and for all species in the earth community. If not addressed, the consequences will become unimaginably worse. Take some time to reflect on the following:

1. For decades, people in wealthy countries have consumed many times the natural resources used by those in impoverished countries and have taken for themselves the resources of other lands. What does that look like? Are these countries overdeveloped? If we live on a limited planet, is it just for a relatively few to consume excessively or to waste resources like water, land, and minerals essential to modern life?

2. Climate change has already had a severe impact on people who have contributed least to carbon emissions. Climate disasters undo decades of improvements and reverse gains in poverty reduction. What obligations do people in the global North have to reduce their carbon emissions when it is those in the global South who will be most severely affected by climate change?

3. For decades, economic growth has been heralded as the solution to every ill, with little recognition that the global economy has to fit within earth's limits. Familiarize yourself with the proposals of ecological economists like Herman Daly and eco-theologians like Sallie McFague, Cynthia Moe-Lobeda, Sean McDonagh, and Leonardo Boff. Is it possible to promote a serious reorientation of the global economy away from growth and toward human development? What beginning steps might help us do that?

The Local: Watershed Discipleship

We recall how deeply grounded the early Franciscan community was to the places of San Damiano and La Portiuncula.

The Franciscan community rebuilt those ruined churches as the material basis for their worship of God, their shared community, and their mission in the world. Congregations and faith communities are invited to explore their connections to land and to a sense of place.

Theologian Ched Myers has articulated a new call to discipleship for our time of ecological crisis. Employing the triple meanings of *watershed discipleship,* Myers interpreted *watershed* first in its common meaning of a decisive turning point, a point of no return. Our planet is in a watershed moment of ecological catastrophe that is bearing down on us in the approaching storm of climate change. We are racing headlong into a future that will degrade the planet's ability to sustain all life. All we have to do to ensure this catastrophic future is to change nothing. Our Christian faith and practice unfold in light of or in spite of this crisis. Our choice is between discipleship and denial. The second dimension of watershed discipleship is the call to relocate ourselves in our watershed, which is the basic habitat unit of all life, including human society. We cannot defend creation in the abstract; we cannot respond to this planetary crisis as a whole. We can only replace ourselves inside the ecological location that defines life—the watershed in which we live. A watershed is like the cupped hands of the Creator forming the "basin of all relations" (The Water Institute, 6), the essential habitat unit that sustains life. It will serve as a lifeboat to carry us through the coming storm. The third dimension of watershed discipleship means becoming students, literally "disciples," of our watershed, becoming literate in its life forms, its ecological dynamics and equilibriums, its treasures, and its wounds.

1. Does your faith community recognize the watershed moment of climate change that defines who we are and what we are called to do? Where do you see evidence of

denial in your own life and in the life of your faith community? Where do you hear a call to faithful watershed discipleship?

2. What is your watershed? What would it mean for you and your community to map your watershed so that you can understand the ecosystems it serves and nourishes? What are the human realities that threaten its well-being? What allies are already working to preserve and protect your watershed? What is being done, for instance, by local voluntary organizations, interfaith groups, and government agencies? What kind of environmental coalitions exist? Do they include people of color?

3. How does the Word of God take on the flesh of this piece of God's earth, your watershed?

4. Living faithfully in this watershed moment demands that environmental sustainability be integral to everything we do as Christian disciples. What specific practices do you now carry out that could be considered watershed practices? How might we reimagine our liturgy like baptism? What about the campus of our local church? Is it water friendly? Do we support and utilize local farms? Is there a nearby stream or a river that is calling for loving stewardship?

5. Living faithfully in this watershed moment demands also that environmental justice be integral to everything we do as Christian disciples. Who are the principal human victims of environmental problems so far in your watershed? Who are likely to be the next victims? How are people of color and low-income people in your watershed affected by environmental issues, and what is their response? Gather information on the environmental justice issues in your watershed, and then identify two of them that deserve priority attention. How can you become more

involved as individuals and as a community? Consider several ways to act: community education, service, use of investments, change in lifestyle, public policy advocacy, and so on.

Epilogue

Francis and the Foolishness of God

Biblical Foundations for the Fool of God

A long tradition of fools exists within the Bible. In the Hebrew scriptures we see Jeremiah parading naked in the streets of Jerusalem to drive home a prophetic point. In the New Testament we first catch sight of John the Baptist wearing a camel skin, eating grasshoppers and honey, hanging out in a desert inhabited only by wild beasts, demons, madmen, and an occasional saint. John is a hard one to follow in this madcap comedy, but the apostles manage to bring the house down. In the ecstatic moment of Pentecost they reel like drunks in the gift of the Holy Spirit.

Jesus himself is the head clown of this tradition, the divine fool who, "despised and rejected," calls us to a different way of being and living in the world, a way fundamentally at odds with the accepted norms of behavior. Jesus is the ultimate fool of God, who fulfills a long prophetic tradition and unleashes a message and a new way of life that the world continues to call foolish, irrational, impractical, and dangerously naive.

The apostle Paul heard this invitation and so began to proclaim this message:

For Christ did not send me to baptize, but to preach the gospel, and not with the wisdom of human eloquence so

that the cross of Christ might not be emptied of its mean-
ing. The message of the cross is foolishness to those who
are perishing, but to us who are being saved it is the power
of God. For it is written, "I will destroy the wisdom of
the wise, and the learning of the learned I will set aside."
Where is the wise one? Where is the scribe? Where is the
debater of this age? Has not God made the wisdom of the
world foolish? For since in the wisdom of God the world
did not come to know God through wisdom, it was the will
of God through the foolishness of the proclamation to save
those who have faith. For Jews demand signs and Greeks
look for wisdom, but we proclaim Christ crucified, a stum-
bling block to Jews and foolishness to Gentiles, but to those
who are called, Jews and Greeks alike, Christ the power
of God and the wisdom of God. For the foolishness of God
is wiser than human wisdom, and the weakness of God is
stronger than human strength. (1 Cor 1:17–25)

Paul called himself and other messengers of the gospel "fools
for Christ." And these fools pursued a path of discipleship in the
world that led to rejection and ridicule, imprisonment, and, for
some like Paul and Peter, even torture and execution by imperial
power. Paul called the message of the gospel a stumbling block
to Jews and folly to Gentiles. But it was not only the message
itself but also the community that gathered around the message
that appeared foolish in Paul's world.

Consider your own call, brothers and sisters: not many
of you were wise by human standards, not many were
powerful, not many were of noble birth. But God chose
what is foolish in the world to shame the wise; God
chose what is weak in the world to shame the strong;
God chose what is low and despised in the world, things

*that are not, to reduce to nothing things that are, so that no
one might boast in the presence of God. (1 Cor 1:26–29)*

Not many are wise, not many are powerful, but God chose
what is foolish and weak to shame the wise and strong. God has
chosen what is foolish in the world to bring down the wise. The
foolishness of God is God's way of working in the world. Using
the most marginalized and disreputable as companions in this
journey toward liberation, God chose the most unlikely instruments for radical change. It is this community of marginalized
people taking on the world with hope, power, and vision that is
the most outlandish thing of all.

THE FOOL IN FRANCIS

The tradition of the fool continues throughout the history of
the church, springing up in different times and places. We see
it in individuals like St. Basil of Russia, who wept with sinners
and denounced the czar, who stole the merchandise of dishonest
merchants, and who threw rocks at the houses of the respectable.
But nowhere do we see this tradition more clearly than we do in
Francis of Assisi.

The worldview of young Francis and his companions was
shaped by a romantic vision of the medieval royal court. The
courtly ideal for Francis was to become a knight, dedicated first
to the service of the king and to a "lady" of the court whose
praises he would sing, whose safety and honor he would vouch-
safe. It is one of those divine ironies that Francis's sense of vocation shifted from this image of the knight in the royal court to
that of the court jester. The fool in the royal court of the Middle
Ages was often derided, the source of amusement, the object
of mockery. But fools served the court in invaluable ways by

mocking the courtly pretensions of power and ambition. Almost everything about the court, even the king, was fair game for the jester because of the tacit agreement that the role of the jester was to remind the court of the limits of its power.

And so Francis became the "fool for Christ," exposing the limitations of the earthly court in the light of Christ. We have reflected on the "foolishness" of Francis in stories of his kissing the leper, giving away money, stripping himself naked, always singing, preaching to animals and birds, accepting ridicule and humiliation joyfully, and seeking the suffering of the cross. We have seen Francis walk unarmed into the enemy's camp, take on the monumental task of rebuilding the church, and risk being transformed himself through deep relationships with the "other." We have reflected upon his willingness to walk to the edge of security, to lose everything in order to be faithful, and to challenge strongly held cultural, economic, and political norms.

Raoul Manselli, a noted biographer of Francis, has pointed out that it was as fools for Christ that Francis and his community were able to evangelize large crowds, not only in Assisi or in Italy, but throughout Europe and beyond. Because the original Franciscan community was limited by the official church to what was called the exhortation for penance, they were not allowed access to the pulpit to preach sermons. Their church was in the streets, squares, marketplaces, and fields. Their congregation comprised ordinary people engaged in everyday life; their medium was a combination of exhortation and theater that struck the popular imagination in a way that learned sermons on Sunday failed to do. As fools for Christ, the friars were prepared to accept the fickleness of those they sought to evangelize.

The most basic inspiration of the Christian tradition of the fool is identification with Christ crucified, active participation in the poverty, nakedness, homelessness, and humiliation of the Lord. The fool is willing to accept the humiliations, risks, ostracism, rejection, and even violence evoked by faithfulness to the gospel and resistance to evil. We have seen how Francis embodied this identification to the point of bearing in his own body the wounds of Christ on the cross. We have seen how Francis lived this identification with the crucified Christ by living in solidarity with the crucified of the world, the marginalized poor. This is the tradition of the fool expressed as the "via negativa," the negative way.

But Francis embodied the "via positiva" as well, the positive way in the tradition of the fool, by his unbounded capacity for joy, his sense of ecstatic union with all things, his sensual delight in the created world, his singing of the Lord's song to all creatures, his sense of the comic and the absurd, his willingness to be the occasion for laughter and amusement, and his gratitude for all things. Francis, as the fool for Christ, united in himself the gospel as both tragedy and comedy.

Foolishness of God
at Work and Play in the World

The Franciscan (and divine) "option for the poor" appears utterly foolish in the context of Western civilization today, fundamentally subversive of the thinking, practice, and power upon which the social order rests. Franciscan foolishness turns on its head all that is called wise by the powerful. Franciscan "weakness" transforms power itself.

Creative appropriation of this foolish way of being in our world requires that we embrace the discipleship journey with abandon. We will experience the subversive joy known by Francis only if we risk embracing the lepers of our day and relinquishing the privilege and wealth that preclude such an embrace. We, too, are invited into dialogue with the ones we know as enemy, with the other, with creation itself, and with our own pain and suffering.

For Jesus and Francis and for ourselves, this foolishness is essentially embodied in the life of the community of believers, fools who know that

• to relinquish the security of possessions in a society unable to take risks only makes sense if our ultimate security rests in God;

• to walk away from the familiar and comfortable in order to follow an unknown path of love and service requires the support of co-believers;

• to believe that we can and must participate in the transformation of the world is best balanced by a loving community that reminds us not to take ourselves too seriously;

• to ask why and to free ourselves from the ideological captivity of a consumer society are only possible when the road is shared.

The fool in our times honors the Creator in all persons and all things, finds profound joy in the possibility of reconciliation across cultural and racial differences, seeks harmony with the rest of the created order, and is a nonviolent promoter of life.

The fool is in the world but not of the world. The fool finds identity not in that which our society acclaims—appearance, accomplishment, affluence, power, consumption—but rather in the discipleship journey toward God.

The fool knows that we and all created things are sacraments of God. The fool believes in and knows by experience the world of the Spirit.

The fool lives in paradise, ridiculing the powers and principalities, because, with Jesus and Francis, the fool in our times remembers the end of the story, the reign of God.

Appendix

A Reflection on the Canticle of Creation

God and All Things

One voice, more than any other in the entire history of the church, has called God's people to praise the Creator who is present in creation. And that voice belongs to St. Francis of Assisi. St. Francis teaches us how to pray with creation. The Canticle of Creation is more than a beautiful poem. It is a spiritual vision of a transformed relationship between humankind and the created order to which we belong. Francis on spiritual retreat in a mountain cave spent an entire night praying "God and all things." That is the essence of Franciscan contemplation—responding to God who is present in all things. Our hope for this meditation is that it will enable us to claim Francis as a spiritual guide who can teach us how to respond to the Loving Creator present in all of creation.

THE CANTICLE OF CREATION

Before we can explore in greater depth the inward ecology of the canticle that greets all creation as brother or sister, we must pause to consider the time and place in which it was written. The culture in which Francis lived made assumptions about certain qualities assigned to each gender that are no longer universally embraced as fixed or inherent. For example, not all cultures consider the sun as a masculine archetype or the moon as a representative symbol of the feminine. To be "lowly" or "humble" is not always a virtue, especially if those characteristics are always attributed to the feminine. To be radiant or powerful cannot always be attributed to the masculine.

In the Canticle of Creation each of the elements is greeted as brother or sister, but in these times we work hard to avoid locking masculine and feminine into closed boxes. As you approach the canticle seek a balance and harmony between the masculine and feminine; allow each cosmic element the opportunity to be different than Francis imagined them. Perhaps by greeting "Sister Sun," rather than "Brother Sun," a woman of faith can reclaim her light-filled being as a shining symbol of divine destiny. Perhaps a man of faith can approach "Brother Moon," rather than "Sister Moon," and undergo a different way of being a masculine child of God. As you read the following meditations on each stanza of the canticle, take one element of the canticle and begin a dialogue with that element. You may want to go to a natural setting that allows you to encounter that element with all of your senses. What deep truth is being invoked in the inward ecology of your soul?

READING THE CANTICLE AS A LENS INTO AN INWARD SPIRITUAL ECOLOGY

Place yourself in a place conducive to meditation, where you can be safe and undisturbed. Do what feels right to consecrate this space, perhaps by lighting a candle or by playing special music. Be comfortable and begin to breathe deeply at a pace that is natural to you. Allow thoughts to come into your mind without judgment on yourself, but just as easily allow those thoughts to move out of your awareness, as if you were lying on the warm ground watching clouds go across the sky. Slowly read each of the following reflections based on the Canticle of Creation and allow yourself to be with each for a time. When you know you are ready, move to the next. (If you are in a group, the reflections can be read successively around the circle.) Listen in your heart to the words of each reflection. Be aware of what images or feelings come up for you.

All praise be yours, my Lord, through Brother Sun . . .
through Sister Sun

Francis finds an inexhaustible source of joy in creation, but this was first and foremost a joy in light. For Francis, the cosmos is an epiphany of light. Even at the end of his life, when he wrote the canticle, at a time when he was almost blind and in agony from an eye condition, Francis still celebrated the light he loved in his poem to Brother Sun and Sister Moon. Francis can teach us how the Sun is the image of the most high God—the divine splendor of the Sun and the abundance it radiates in the heavens. For Francis, the Sun symbolizes the sovereign reality that draws the soul toward it. The Sun calls out to that which is deepest and most divine in us. The Sun draws our gaze within to a vision of ourselves as light-filled beings. The Sun is a glimpse of our own destiny to be transformed. Dialogue with the Sun raises questions for us, such as where is my vocation calling me? Where is my life going? What is the vision of my own transformation that guides my journey? We all need to pray with the Sun in order to reclaim a vision of transformation, as individuals, as people of faith and indeed as the human family.

All praise be yours, my Lord, through Sisters Moon and Stars . . . through Brothers Moon and Stars

Our dialogue with Sun helps us to imagine our light-filled destiny, our transformed future. What does Moon have to teach us? The story is told of Francis that late one night he woke up the entire town of Assisi by ringing the cathedral bell that was used only for the direst emergencies. The townspeople flooded out of their homes only to find that crazy fool Francis summoning them to see the beautiful moonrise over the Umbrian plain. Similarly, Francis summons us. Whenever we see the Moon rising in an evening, let us offer a prayer that we might learn from the Moon. The Moon has much to teach us about how to move through the cycles of waxing and waning as the process that carries us toward our own transformation. The Moon teaches us about what it means to approach life as mystery, about how to accept the parts of our hearts that remain troubled, unknown, or unresolved. If the Sun embodies our divine transformation, the Moon shows us the way through death and resurrection, through letting go and letting be. The Moon can teach us about letting go of what holds us back and letting be all that has a right to life alongside of ours. All praise be yours, my Lord, through our brother and sister, Sun and Moon. We join with all God's creatures on this planet in this hymn of praise for our Creator.

All praise be yours, my Lord, through Brothers Wind and Air . . . through Sisters Wind and Air

Francis's invocation of Wind and Air is an image for God that has deep biblical roots, beginning with the Hebrew word *ruach*, which is a feminine noun in the Hebrew language. *Ruach,* the Hebrew word for "spirit," is loosely translated "wind," "breath," or even "storm." With *ruach* translated "breath," we are reminded of the fundamental interaction of all creatures. As we breathe, we interact with the energy of the universe in a very tangible and necessary way—a basic reality of which we are largely unconscious. To become more aware of our breathing can help us recover a sense of groundedness in our bodies, ourselves, our universe. The more we learn about the life of the spirit, the simpler it seems to get. The most elemental lesson of the spiritual life is the question of how we breathe. We are better able to locate and live out of a spiritual center if we first become aware of our breathing, doing it more deeply and rhythmically. Perhaps this is the most basic lesson about the spiritual life, as basic as each and every breath we take. Our physical life depends on the natural rhythm of our breathing from moment to moment. Just so, our spiritual lives depend on this centered inspiration of the Holy Spirit in each and every moment and the exhalation of anxiety, fear, and ill will.

But *ruach* can also be translated "wind." What does it mean when we speak of the Spirit of God as Wind? The first time that we encounter this description of Spirit in the scriptures is in the creation story in Genesis. Do you recall that beautiful poetic description of the creative moment in Genesis 1: "And the Spirit of God hovered over the face of the Deep?" The verb used here, the Hebrew word loosely translated "hover," is used primarily to describe the flight of a mother bird who circles above the nest of her young. It is as if the Hebrew poet is saying that in the crisis of the creative moment, the Wind of the Spirit hovers above, watching out for us like a mother bird protecting her young. We also recall Jesus's words: "The wind blows where it will" (John 3:8). It cannot be contained or even seen, but it is known by its effects. Our greatest temptation is to try to trap the Holy Spirit in a box.

Ruach can also be translated "storm." The Spirit as storm came to Job in the turbulence and intensity of the whirlwind. The Spirit is not some domesticated fuzzy feeling but can come to us in the wildness of the Storm of God. Remember the last time you were up close to a storm. Remember that rush of feeling that was both dread and excitement. Consider what it would be like to encounter the Holy Spirit in the same way. When Francis extols Wind and Air he evokes images of the Spirit, of great change, conversion, new inspiration, freedom, and creativity— apt metaphors for Francis's whole life. His freedom in the Spirit led him to live in a space that was profoundly countercultural and simultaneously prophetic.

All praise be yours, my Lord, through Sister Water . . . through Brother Water

It was St. Francis who brought the church back to awareness of the presence of the Creator in all creation, especially in Water. St. Francis can teach us to pray with creation and with Water as we find ourselves alongside a mountain stream, swimming in a lake, or walking along a beach in the mighty presence of the ocean. We do not have to live in the desert to understand that life depends on Water. Water is life. Water is a powerful element that can carve canyons from solid rock. Yet Water is fluid, taking many shapes and forms. Water is clear and transparent, open to shining and dancing light. To live under the sign of our baptism is to be in prayerful dialogue with Water. In dialogue with Brother Water we might ask ourselves: How might I, like Water, surrender more freely in service to the Creator? How might I, like Water, nurture life in others? As our Creator gives Water to me, how can I give myself in service to others? What canyons can I carve through the destructive values of our culture?

All praise be yours, my Lord, through Brother Fire . . . through Sister Fire

Picture the Franciscan community rebuilding a ruined chapel by a great forest, next to an open plain. There are small huts made of sticks and rocks, wood, and brush. Fire was a familiar sight in the Franciscan community because, of course, meals were cooked on a campfire. If you have ever sat by the fireplace or at a campfire and been mesmerized by the dancing flames, you know something of the ability of Fire to speak to the human heart. Fire has deep roots as a biblical symbol. There is the burning bush of Moses, which symbolizes the divine pathos of the Creator, who is moved by the cries of slaves and enters history to liberate them. In Jesus own words: "I have come to set the world on fire, and how I wish it were already burning" (Luke 12:49). The early followers of Jesus were anointed by the Holy Spirit at Pentecost, and it seemed as though flames danced upon their heads. Blaise Pascal, the great mathematician, physicist, and Christian writer, noted in his journal on November 23, 1654, that he could describe his intense experience in prayer only as Fire. Poets and mystics like Gerard Manley Hopkins have experienced this divine Fire erupting in all things created. In one poem Hopkins wrote that "as kingfishers catch fire, dragonflies draw flame."

In the eyes of the poet and the person of faith, everything glows with the fiery energy of the Divine. When one of Francis's early followers, a brother by the name of Giovanni, listened to Francis speak of God, he felt his heart would melt like wax near a fire. And the love of God so inflamed him that he could not stand still and endure it. He would get up and, as if drunk in the Spirit, would wander about the garden, the woods, the church, talking as the flame moved him. Throughout the ages, Fire has been a symbol of Eros, of love seeking union with the beloved. Fire has been the metaphor of transformation. Earlier we explored the great love between Francis and Clare, his spiritual sister. Clare came to visit Francis one day, and into the evening, around the campfire, they engaged in holy and passionate conversation about their love of God and creation. That very night the people of Assisi looked beyond the walls of the town, across the plain, and toward the forest where the Franciscan community lived. They saw a red and orange glow as if a great fire were raging. They rushed out of the city to put out the fire only to discover Francis and Clare sitting and talking to one another.

Imagine that we are among those gathered around the campfire with Francis and Clare; Sun is setting to the west and Moon is rising over the mountains. The coolness of the evening is wonderfully offset by Fire, which warms our feet and dances in our eyes. Francis and Clare invite us to dialogue with Fire. Francis and Clare ask us to consider the source of passion in our lives. What are we passionate about? Where do we find energy? What is our deepest joy? Are we moving toward it? It might be that we are experiencing the consuming power of Fire in a time of suffering or trial. In our dialogue with Fire, it may be that the most important thing we need to do is to name and acknowledge our anger. This anger might be from the past or from a situation being experienced right now. It may be anger at the folly of humankind in our wanton destruction of our planet or callous disregard for the poor. The Fire of anger within us can be destructive or creative. The Fire within us can cause havoc, or it can purify us and lead us toward transformation. What about your passion for justice, our longing for peace? Perhaps that fiery passion is only a faintly glowing ember right now. Can we gently fan it until it reignites? Francis and Clare invite us to be in dialogue with the Fire within each of us. How do we befriend Fire, who comes to us in suffering, in mystery, in love?

All praise be yours, my Lord, through Sister Earth, our mother . . . through Brother Earth, our father

We can imagine Francis crying out in joy as he trekked across the landscape where he was born, lived, and died—Assisi. The area around Assisi in North Central Italy is a place of amazing beauty to this day. Assisi is surrounded by a stunning landscape of agricultural plains, old-growth forest, and craggy mountain ranges. As a youth Francis would be gone for days, wandering the forests or hillsides. There is no doubt that the geography of that place shaped and formed his soul. What was true for Francis is probably true for all of us—that the place on Earth where we grew up or live now will have a formative impact on the geography of our own souls. How does the particular geography of my place shape me? Francis had a great love for the Earth. In the Canticle of Creation, Earth is preeminent as mother but is still our sister as part of creation. For Francis to abide with Earth was to participate in Earth's life, to get dirty in planting and harvesting the bounty of the land. Following the example of their leader, the early Franciscans worked in the fields alongside the farmers; in effect, they became migrant workers who accepted whatever the farmer would give them for their daily bread. Francis was actually fond of spending time in caves in the mountains around Assisi as a way of being closer to the Earth he loved. Caves were for him perhaps something akin to what the kivas were and are for Native American peoples across the Desert Southwest. To be in a cave was for Francis to descend into the archeology of our origins, to reconnect with the womb that gave us birth. But going into the cave was also a way to remind himself that we are humble creatures of dust. In the cave Francis faced his own mortal creatureliness.

In this stanza Francis cries out in thanksgiving for the dazzling feast at the table of creation. Earth nourishes and sustains us with all good things. We are from Earth, who has given birth to us. Too long we have denied you who give us life. Our very bodies are a gift from you. How can we forget that in every moment our lives depend on you? Teach us never to try to dominate you but in humility to receive your gifts and care. Help us to heal the painful wound that we have inflicted on you and on ourselves. Praise be yours, Sister Earth.

All Praise be yours, my Lord,
through those who grant pardon for love of you,
through those who endure sickness and trial

With this stanza of the canticle we remember the conquest imposed upon Native American peoples, and we ask, first, not who will grant us pardon, but how we will actively repent for our relentless domination of nature. To repent is to change direction. What Columbus stumbled upon and claimed as an unknown continent may have been, at least according to some scholars, more populous than Europe, with bigger cities, more advanced medicine, superior agriculture, and healthier people. From the moment Europeans arrived here, indigenous peoples began to resist that conquest. The century following discovery led to more environmental destruction than the ten centuries prior. For more than five hundred years indigenous peoples have been resisting conquest, struggling to survive as a people, to protect their culture, and to preserve the earth, which is the very basis of their identity. A few years ago at a continent-wide gathering of progressive Christians in Latin America, Gustavo Gutiérrez, the father of liberation theology, said that five hundred years ago Christian Europe came to America and encountered indigenous peoples; in that first encounter they did not listen to or honor or respect our Native brothers and sisters. Instead they participated in the conquest of indigenous people and the destruction of their way of life.

Now it is time for a second encounter *(encuentro)* in which we truly listen and learn to understand how Native American peoples see and experience the divine Spirit moving and working in this world. This second *encuentro* between the church and indigenous peoples is beginning to happen. Indigenous communities are suffering tremendously, but there is something in their relatedness to the earth that has allowed them to continue to affirm life and to continue the struggle in hope. We have much to learn from this.

All praise be yours, my Lord, through Sister Death . . . through Brother Death

When the moment of his death approached, Francis asked to be stripped naked and placed on the ground, with his brothers and sisters singing the Canticle of Creation. Through the natural process of aging our bodies wear out, break down. There may come a time in our life's journey when we desire to be liberated from the limitations of our fragile, finite body. Many of us have little awareness of our body until something goes wrong with it. Anyone who has ever known illness or injury knows that we live inside bodies that are vulnerable to pain and suffering. The ultimate health issue is the death of the body. When the moment of our death approaches, we hope that the words "ashes to ashes, dust to dust" will not feel like a mournful cry. We hope that one day these words will be heard as a joyous offering up of the body to return to the earth to which all life belongs. Francis meditating in the cave is a reminder to us that it is a mature faith that can contemplate our own mortality and the reality of physical death. Here a question is rightly posed: Why does the church stubbornly reaffirm this belief in the resurrection of the body? It would be so much more neat and tidy if we believed in the Greek idea of the immortality of the soul—that at the moment of death the soul leaves behind the finite body and goes to be with God. But that is not what Christianity teaches. Christian faith teaches that our bodies are a sign of our solidarity with the created order, our fundamental connectedness with all of nature. Christianity teaches that when we die, our hope is not in the inherent immortality of the soul; rather, our hope is in the resurrection of the body and of all creation. We believe in the resurrection of the body because through our bodies we will participate in the resurrection of the entire creation, a new creation, transformed and reunited with the Creator.

CONTINUING TO PRAY WITH CREATION

When all the reflections have been read, either in silence by yourself or with the group, make a few notes in a journal about which element of the canticle speaks to you. If you are in a group, allow some time for discussion. When you have thought about the element that seems to be speaking to you, consider how you might continue the dialogue. If it is Sun, plan to be present at a sunrise or sunset in the next week. If it is Water, return to a lake or stream that you have enjoyed in the past. Perhaps it will be some element not included in the canticle. Whichever element you choose, design for yourself a mini-retreat, a meditative encounter with that element of creation as the focus of your contemplation.

When you have decided how to place yourself before this element, go through the steps of allowing yourself to be comfortable and at rest. Breathe deeply. Perhaps you may want to read again the prayer from the canticle or some other reading that seems appropriate. When you have allowed yourself to absorb all the sensations of that element, turn deeply within. What is this element saying to you? Why do you feel you have been drawn to this particular element? What interior reality does this cosmic element represent in you? In spoken words or by journaling, whatever is comfortable for you, carry on a free-flowing dialogue with Sun or Moon, Water or Fire, Wind or Earth, or whatever element you have chosen. You may find that the element is evoking in you growth and transformation.

The element that you choose for the meditation will undoubtedly change from time to time, as your own contemplative process carries you to new questions of identity and change. Be willing to experiment, to be a "fool" for God as you learn more and more how to pray with creation.

Bibliography

Armstrong, Regis J., OFM Cap., Wayne Hellman, OFM Conv., and William Short, OFM. *Francis of Assisi: Early Documents*, vol. 2: *The Founder* (Hyde Park, NY: New City Press, 2000).

Bernard of Clairvaux. "In Praise of the New Knighthood: A Treatise on the Knights Templar and the Holy Places of Jerusalem," Cistercian Fathers Series, no. 19b (Kalamazoo, MI: Cistercian Publications, 1977).

Berry, Wendell. "Christianity and The Survival of Creation," in *Sex, Economy, Freedom and Community: Eight Essays* (New York: Random House, 1992).

Boff, Leonardo. *Cry of the Earth, Cry of the Poor* (Maryknoll, NY: Orbis Books, 1997).

———. *Ecology and Liberation: A New Paradigm* (Maryknoll, NY: Orbis Books, 1993).

———. *Saint Francis, A Model for Human Liberation* (Maryknoll, NY: Orbis Books, 2006).

St. Bonaventure. "Major Life of St. Francis." In *St. Francis of Assisi: Writings and Early Biographies*, ed. Marion Habig, English Omnibus of the Sources for the Life of St. Francis, vol. 1 (Chicago: Franciscan Herald Press, 1991).

Brown, Raphael, ed. and trans. *The Little Flowers of St. Francis* (New York: Image Books, 1958).

Brussat, Frederic and Mary Ann. *Spiritual Literacy: Reading the Sacred in Everyday Life* (New York: Touchstone–Simon and Schuster, 1996).

Butigan, Ken, Mary Litell, OSF, and Louis Vitale, OFM. *Franciscan Nonviolence: Stories, Reflections, Principles, Practices, and Resources* (Las Vegas: Pace e Bene Nonviolence Service, 2003).

Celano, Thomas of. "The First Life of St. Francis." Translation taken from M. L. Cameron, *The Inquiring Pilgrim's Guide to Assisi*, trans.

A. G. Ferrers Howell (London, 1926). Original language: Latin. The text, available at http://www.indiana.edu/~dmdhist/francis. htm#1.6, was prepared for the web by Prof. Leah Shopkow and is reprinted with her permission.

―――. "St. Francis of Assisi: Second Life." In *St. Francis of Assisi: Writings and Early Biographies*, ed. Marion Habig, English Omnibus of the Sources for the Life of St. Francis, vol. 1 (Chicago: Franciscan Herald Press, 1991).

Chenoweth, Erica, and Maria Stephan. *Why Civil Resistance Works* (New York: Columbia University Press, 2011).

Cusato, Michael F. "From Damietta to LaVerna: The Impact on Francis of His Experience in Egypt." In *Daring to Embrace Each Other: Francis and Muslims in Dialogue,* ed. Sr. Daira Mitchell OSF, *Spirit and Life* 12 (2008).

Domhoff, G. William. "Wealth, Income, and Power." Sociology Department, University of California at Santa Cruz. First posted September 2005; most recently updated February 2013. http://whorulesamerica.net/power/wealth.html.

St. Francis. "Admonitions." In *St. Francis of Assisi: Writings and Early Biographies*, ed. Marion Habig, English Omnibus of the Sources for the Life of St Francis, vol. 1 (Chicago: Franciscan Herald Press, 1991).

St. Francis. "Rule of 1221." In *St. Francis of Assisi: Writings and Early Biographies*, ed. Marion Habig, English Omnibus of the Sources for the Life of St. Francis, vol. 1 (Chicago: Franciscan Herald Press, 1991).

―――. "Rule of 1223." In *St. Francis of Assisi: Writings and Early Biographies*, ed. Marion Habig, English Omnibus of the Sources for the Life of St. Francis, vol. 1 (Chicago: Franciscan Herald Press, 1991).

Gutiérrez, Gustavo. *A Theology of Liberation* (Maryknoll, NY: Orbis Books, 1973).

Hauerwas, Stanley. "Prologue." In Michael Long, *Christian Peace and Nonviolence* (Maryknoll, NY: Orbis Books, 2011).

Haught, John F. *Christianity and Science: Toward a Theology of Nature* (Maryknoll, NY: Orbis Books, 2007).

Hawken, Paul. *Blessed Unrest: How the Largest Movement in the World Came into Being and Why No One Saw It Coming* (New York: Viking Press, 2007).

Holland, Joe, and Peter Henriot. *Social Analysis: Linking Faith and Justice* (Maryknoll, NY: Orbis Books, 1983).

Jenkins, Philip. *The Next Christendom: The Coming of Global Christianity* (Oxford: Oxford University Press, 2007).

Johnson, Elizabeth. *The Quest for the Living God: Mapping Frontiers in the Theology of God* (New York: Continuum, 2007).

Jörgensen, Johannes. *St. Francis of Assisi* (New York: Image Books, 1955).

Kavanaugh, John. *Still Following Christ in a Consumer Society* (Maryknoll, NY: Orbis Books, 1991).

Leclerc, Eloi. *The Canticle of Creatures: Symbols of Union* (Chicago: Franciscan Herald Press, 1977).

Long, Michael. *Christian Peace and Nonviolence* (Maryknoll, NY: Orbis Books, 2011).

Marini, Alfonso. "Francis of Assisi and Islam." *Spirit and Life* (Maltese Franciscans) 106 (2013).

Manselli, Raoul. *St. Francis of Assisi* (Chicago: Franciscan Herald Press, 1988).

McFague, Sallie. *The Body of God: An Ecological Theology* (Minneapolis: Fortress Press, 1993).

———. *A New Climate For Theology: God, The World, and Global Warming* (Minneapolis: Fortress Press, 2008).

Mead, Loren. *The Once and Future Church* (Durham, NC: Alban Institute, 2001).

Mitchell, Stephen. *The Gospel According to Jesus* (New York: Harper Collins, 1991).

Moe-Lobeda, Cynthia. *Healing a Broken World: Globalization and God* (Minneapolis: Fortress Press, 2002).

———. *Resisting Structural Evil: Love as Ecological-Economic Vocation* (Minneapolis: Fortress Press, 2013).

Moses, Paul. *The Saint and the Sultan* (New York: Doubleday, 2009).

Myers, Ched. *Binding the Strong Man: A Political Reading of Mark's Story of Jesus* (Maryknoll, NY: Orbis Books, 1988).

Pope Francis, *The Joy of the Gospel (Evangelii gaudium)* (2013). www.vatican.va.

Pope John XXIII, *Peace on Earth (Pacem in terris)* (1963). www.vatican.va.

Pope Paul VI, *Declaration on the Relationship of the Church to Non-Christian Religions* (1965). www.vatican.va.

Roche, Douglas. *Peacemakers: How People Around the World Are Building a World Free of War* (Toronto: Lorimer, 2014).

Rynne, Terence. *Jesus Christ, Peacemaker* (Maryknoll, NY: Orbis Books, 2014).

Sagan, Carl. *Cosmos* (Ballantine, 1985; original Random House, 1980).

Sims, Rev. Bennett J. *Servanthood: Leadership for the Third Millennium* (Boston: Cowley Publications, 1997).

Sobrino, Jon. *Christology at the Crossroads* (Maryknoll, NY: Orbis Books, 1978).

———. *Where Is God?* (Maryknoll, NY: Orbis Books, 2004).

Tickle, Phyllis. *The Great Emergence* (Grand Rapids, MI: Baker Books, 2012).

Water Institute. *Basin of Relations: A Citizen's Guide to Protecting and Restoring our Watersheds*, Occidental Art and Ecology Center (Occidental, CA).

WCC (World Council of Churches). *Just Peace Companion*, 2d ed. (Geneva: WCC Publications, 2012).